BARRON'S BOOK NOTES

JOHN STEINBECK'S

Of Mice and Men

BY

Michael Goodman
Editor
Scholastic Inc.

SERIES EDITOR

Michael Spring
Editor, *Literary Cavalcade*
Scholastic Inc.

BARRON'S EDUCATIONAL SERIES, INC.
Woodbury, New York / London / Toronto / Sydney

004145093

ACKNOWLEDGMENTS

We would like to acknowledge the many painstaking hours of work Holly Hughes and Thomas F. Hirsch have devoted to making the *Book Notes* series a success.

All inquiries should be addressed to:
Barron's Educational Series, Inc.
113 Crossways Park Drive
Woodbury, New York 11797

Library of Congress Catalog Card No. 84-18418

International Standard Book No. 0-8120-3431-7   ·

Library of Congress Cataloging in Publication Data
Goodman, Michael.
    John Steinbeck's Of mice and men.

    (Barron's book notes)
    Bibliography: p. 81
    Summary: A guide to reading "Of Mice and Men" with
a critical and appreciative mind. Includes background
on the author's life and times, sample tests, term
paper suggestions, and a reading list.
    1. Steinbeck, John, 1902–1968. Of mice and men.
    [1. Steinbeck, John, 1902–1968. Of mice and men.
    2. American literature—History and criticism]   I. Title.
II. Series.
PS3537.T3234O43   1984   813'.52   84-18418
ISBN 0-8120-3431-7

PRINTED IN THE UNITED STATES OF AMERICA

456   550   98765432

CONTENTS

ADVISORY BOARD

HOW TO USE THIS BOOK

You have to know how to approach literature in order to get the most out of it. This *Barron's Book Notes* volume follows a plan based on methods used by some of the best students to read a work of literature.

Begin with the guide's section on the author's life and times. As you read, try to form a clear picture of the author's personality, circumstances, and motives for writing the work. This background usually will make it easier for you to hear the author's tone of voice, and follow where the author is heading.

Then go over the rest of the introductory material—such sections as those on the plot, characters, setting, themes, and style of the work. Underline, or write down in your notebook, particular things to watch for, such as contrasts between characters and repeated literary devices. At this point, you may want to develop a system of symbols to use in marking your text as you read. (Of course, you should only mark up a book you own, not one that belongs to another person or a school.) Perhaps you will want to use a different letter for each character's name, a different number for each major theme of the book, a different color for each important symbol or literary device. Be prepared to mark up the pages of your book as you read. Put your marks in the margins so you can find them again easily.

Now comes the moment you've been waiting for—the time to start reading the work of literature. You may want to put aside your *Barron's Book Notes* volume until you've read the work all the way through. Or you may want to alternate, reading the *Book Notes* analysis of each section as soon as you have finished reading the corresponding part of the original. Before you move on, reread crucial passages you don't fully understand. (Don't take this guide's analysis for granted—make up your own mind as to what the work means.)

Once you've finished the whole work of literature, you may want to review it right away, so you can firm up your ideas about what it means. You may want to leaf through the book concentrating on passages you marked in reference to one character or one theme. This is also a good time to reread the *Book Notes* introductory material, which pulls together insights on specific topics.

When it comes time to prepare for a test or to write a paper, you'll already have formed ideas about the work. You'll be able to go back through it, refreshing your memory as to the author's exact words and perspective, so that you can support your opinions with evidence drawn straight from the work. Patterns will emerge, and ideas will fall into place; your essay question or term paper will almost write itself. Give yourself a dry run with one of the sample tests in the guide. These tests present both multiple-choice and essay questions. An accompanying section gives answers to the multiple-choice questions as well as suggestions for writing the essays. If you have to select a term paper topic, you may choose one from the list of suggestions in this book. This guide also provides you with a reading list, to help you when you start research for a term paper, and a selection of provocative comments by critics, to spark your thinking before you write.

THE AUTHOR AND HIS TIMES

John Steinbeck always planned to be a writer. He was basically a shy person; he rarely granted interviews and felt a little uncomfortable as he gained more fame and publicity. He didn't really enjoy face-to-face contact, even with his friends, and never felt he communicated well over the telephone. Steinbeck was most at ease when he was writing. In his lifetime, he wrote thousands of letters (sometimes even six or seven a day), 16 novels, one short story collection, eight works of nonfiction, and two filmscripts.

Steinbeck's favorite instrument was the pencil. He would start each day with 24 newly sharpened pencils and would need to sharpen them again before the day was through. He wrote in a tiny script, usually on yellow legal-size pads. Little by little, however, his pencils gave way to a typewriter on which he continued to pound out letters and prose at a remarkable pace.

Steinbeck never wrote an autobiography, but all of his writing contains pieces of his life story. The settings of most of the books are the areas near Salinas and Monterey, in California, where Steinbeck was born and lived most of his life. He came from a working-class background, and most of his characters have to struggle to make a living. Before he began making enough money to live on with his writing, Steinbeck worked as a ranch hand, bricklayer, fruit picker, and marine biologist. He worked with union members and with migrant laborers. These people became the focus of his most important writing. And all of his experiences helped to mold the plots and themes of his books.

Steinbeck's early novels were also conceived in the 1930s during the Great Depression. Poverty and rootlessness seem to hang over the lives of Steinbeck's characters. Perhaps this mirrors not only the period of time but also the author's own struggles to find a place in which he could write, and an audience to recognize and appreciate his writings.

Steinbeck was born in Salinas on February 27, 1902. His father was a farmer and treasurer of Monterey County. His mother was a schoolteacher in Salinas. From his mother, Steinbeck learned to love books— among his favorites were *Crime and Punishment, Paradise Lost*, and *Le Morte d'Arthur* (the first book he ever owned). He also loved to read the King James version of the Bible. As you will soon see, the last three of these books are echoed in interesting ways in *Of Mice and Men*.

Besides books, Steinbeck had another great love while he was growing up—nature. He worked on farms and ranches during his high-school vacations and developed a closeness to the land and the plants and creatures that lived on it. This sensitivity toward nature found its place in Steinbeck's writings, particularly *The Red Pony, The Pastures of Heaven*, and *Of Mice and Men*. In each of these works Steinbeck's natural settings are places of both life and death, places that allow human beings to enter them but refuse to be dominated by human beings. Such a place is the spot along the banks of the Salinas River where the opening and closing scenes of *Of Mice and Men* occur. This setting is alive, but death always lurks nearby. Within the novel, it serves as both a haven and a burial ground. Although Steinbeck studied nature and natural forces, his real focus was always people. Steinbeck was a careful observer and listener. His books are noted for the accuracy of their characters and language. For example, the bunk house in *Of Mice and Men* comes alive for readers because of Steinbeck's understanding of the patterns of the ranch hands' lives and the rhythms of their speech. He had, after all, lived these patterns and rhythms himself.

Steinbeck's critics have sometimes accused him of being too careful and objective in his presentation of his characters and stories. They have complained that the writer was too much of a scientific observer (the marine biologist side of him) and did not feel or present enough real emotion in his works. As you read *Of Mice and Men*, you'll have to decide for yourself whether Steinbeck is genuinely sympathetic toward his characters and their troubles or whether he has chosen merely to sit back and watch them in their hopeless struggle to improve their lives.

Steinbeck's career can generally be broken down into three periods: 1) the years before fame (1929–34); 2) the years of growing fame (1935–45); and 3) the years of continued popularity (the period after World War II until his death in 1968). *Of Mice and Men* was written during the middle period, along with Steinbeck's most famous work, *The Grapes of Wrath*. The period between the Depression and World War II was a bittersweet time in the United States; Steinbeck's writings reflect the sense of loneliness and desperation many Americans felt. The books are sad but truthful, and they won immediate and lasting public approval.

Steinbeck published his first novel, *Cup of Gold*, in 1929. It failed to earn back the $250 the publisher had given the author as an advance. Steinbeck was not really surprised by the book's failure. In one of his letters he wrote that he didn't expect to be "above average" until his fifth book. As it turned out, Steinbeck underestimated himself. His fourth book, *Tortilla Flat*, published in 1935, won him public acceptance and critical attention. It also earned some money for him. Steinbeck received between $3000 and $4000 for the film rights to *Tortilla Flat*. For a man used to earning $35 a week, this seemed like a fortune. Steinbeck determined to get even more serious about his writing: his career was entering its second phase.

Two years later, he published *Of Mice and Men*. It was a Book-of-the-Month Club selection and earned Steinbeck the honor of being named one of the Ten Outstanding Young Men of the Year.

The book was not an easy one to write. Steinbeck determined to create a new literature form with it. He called this form a *play-novelette*, a short novel that contained the sparseness of language and description of a play. (You can read more about this form in the Form and Structure section of this guide.) Steinbeck expected problems getting the form just right, but there was one problem he didn't anticipate—one night while he and his wife were out, their Irish Setter puppy found the manuscript and destroyed nearly half of it. It took Steinbeck two months to re-create the missing parts.

As soon as Steinbeck finished the book, he immediately began work on a play version of the story which had a successful run on Broadway in 1938. The author was not in attendance on opening night instead he was living in a migrant camp in Oklahoma He was developing the first-hand insights for his most important work, *The Grapes of Wrath*, published the next year. *The Grapes of Wrath* was powerful, controversial, and, most of all, popular. It was the best-selling book of 1939 and one of the top sellers of 1940 as well. Steinbeck's portrayal of a family of displaced Oklahoma farmers plagued by elements of nature and human injustice won him both fame and hatred. He even received several threats on his life. A Congressman called the book "a black, infernal creation of a distorted mind," while Steinbeck's peers awarded him both the Pulitzer Prize and the American Booksellers' Award. Over half a million copies of the original edition were sold.

None of Steinbeck's later works could match the sharpness of *Of Mice and Men* or the power and scope of *The Grapes of Wrath*, but they earned him fame and money nonetheless. The author remained very popular with the public but fell out of critical favor for a while. Recently, however, his works have found revival on television, in movies, and on stage.

Following the publication of his last novel, *The Winter of Our Discontent*, Steinbeck was awarded the Nobel Prize for Literature in 1962. The award noted Steinbeck's "great feeling for nature, for the tilled soil, the wasteland, the mountains, and the ocean coasts . . . in the midst of and beyond the world of human beings."

Perhaps the clearest embodiment of Steinbeck's feelings for nature and his careful observation of our place within the natural scheme of things is in *Of Mice and Men*. The book is Steinbeck's statement of the pain of human loneliness and the struggle of man to find a home within the "fat of the land." The book has remained popular not because the novel is hopeful or happy (it isn't), but because, like all of Steinbeck's writings, it rings true and clear.

THE NOVEL

The Plot

Two traveling laborers, George Milton and Lennie Small, are on their way to a job loading barley at a California ranch. It is a Friday evening, and they decide to spend the night out in the open along the banks of the Salinas River before reporting to the ranch the next morning.

As the two men begin discussing their plans, the contrasts between them become apparent. George is small and quick and does all of the thinking and talking for the pair. Lennie is big and slow witted. Lennie follows George's words and actions like a younger brother or a faithful dog.

The two men have been traveling together for some time, and Lennie seems always to get them into trouble. Lennie likes to pet soft things. These things range from the dead mouse George takes away from Lennie in the first scene of the book, to the soft dresses of young women. We learn that Lennie's touching a girl's dress forced them to flee from their last job in the town of Weed.

Over a dinner of canned beans, George fills Lennie in on their new jobs and sets down some rules. Lennie is not to say anything; he is to avoid trouble; and he is to come back to the riverbank, hide, and wait for George should trouble arise. Lennie then asks George to repeat his explanation of why the two men are different from other migrant workers and how they will have a farm of their own someday on which Lennie will get to tend rabbits. George starts out his explanation in a bored tone, but little by little his enthusiasm grows with Lennie's. The two men go to sleep in a happy mood within a peaceful natural setting.

The next morning they appear at the ranch where they are greeted by an old man named Candy and his old dog. Candy fills them in on the ranch and its personalities. Then their boss comes into the bunk house. He is angry that George and Lennie weren't around for the morning work shift. George lies that they were given wrong directions by a bus driver. George continues to answer all of the questions the boss asks, even those directed toward Lennie. The boss is suspicious. When Lennie does repeat one of George's comments in his unintelligent way, George glares at him and later scolds him.

The boss' son Curley, a quick-tempered bully, comes into the bunk house looking for his father. Curley questions the new men and tries to pick a fight with Lennie. George is nervous about the potential dangers that Curley presents and warns Lennie to stay away from him. He repeats his instructions for Lennie to hide in the brush along the riverbank if there should be any trouble.

In walks Curley's wife, supposedly looking for her husband but really attempting to greet the new men and show off her good looks. George and Candy put her down, but Lennie defends her. George warns Lennie to avoid her totally. Lennie also seems apprehensive now and wants to leave right away. "It's mean here," he says. George tells him they will leave as soon as they have a little more of a stake together with which to purchase their own farm.

Slim, the authority figure of the bunk house, walks in next. He is interested in the fact that George and Lennie travel together, a rare situation among ranch hands. Slim also announces that his dog has had a litter of puppies. Slim and another ranch hand, Carlson, discuss the idea of killing Candy's old dog and giving him one of the new puppies instead. George agrees to ask Slim if Lennie can have one of the puppies.

While talking to Slim in the bunk house later that day, George describes his relationship with Lennie. He admits that Lennie isn't bright, but he is a nice guy. Lennie provides companionship and makes George feel smart alongside him. When Lennie walks into the bunk house with his puppy hidden under his shirt, George prophetically warns Lennie that handling the pup so much might kill it.

As all the men gather in the bunk house, Carlson begins pressuring Candy to let him put his dog out of its misery. He explains that he will shoot the dog in the back of the head so it will feel no pain. When Slim joins in the pressuring, Candy finally gives in. Later, Candy overhears George telling Lennie once again about the farm and the rabbits. He asks to be part of the venture and offers to advance half of the money they need to buy the farm. Suddenly the impossible dream seems within reach. Candy confides to George that he should have shot his dog himself, not let a stranger do the task.

Curley walks in, looking for his wandering wife. When he spots Lennie still smiling from the memory of his rabbits, Curley thinks the big man is making fun of him. He begins taunting and hitting Lennie, who refuses to fight back until George tells him to. Then Lennie grabs Curley's hand and begins flipping the smaller man about until he crushes his hand.

Later that night, while George and some of the others are in town at a whorehouse, Lennie comes into the room of Crooks, the black stable worker. Crooks at first objects to this invasion of his privacy, but Lennie's innocent good humor wins him over. Crooks describes the difficulties of being a black man on the ranch, and Lennie talks about the future farm. When Candy comes in and tells that he has offered to put up some of the money, Crooks asks to be included, too. Curley's wife, looking for company, also invades Crooks' sanctum. Crooks and Candy argue with her, but she begins playing up to Lennie. She leaves when George comes in. George is annoyed to learn that Lennie and Candy have shared the dream with someone else.

The next afternoon, all of the trouble that George predicted begins to come true. Lennie has handled his puppy too much and has broken its neck. As he tries to hide the animal, Curley's wife comes into the barn. She talks to Lennie about her life and seems to be seducing him. When she learns that Lennie likes soft things, she invites him to touch her hair. He does so, but, as always, holds on too tight. The woman begins to struggle and yell, and Lennie panics, breaking her neck just as he had done to the puppy. After Lennie flees, Candy finds the woman's body. He gets George and asks for reassurance that the two of them can make the dream of the farm come true, even without Lennie. But George has already forsaken the vision. He asks Candy to give him a few minutes' headstart before telling the others. In that time, George steals Carlson's Luger, the same gun that was used to kill Candy's dog. George reenters the barn with the others to discover the body, and he tries to convince the men that Lennie should only be put away because he meant no harm. But Curley insists on a lynching, and they go out looking for Lennie.

The final scene occurs on the same riverbank where the book opened. Lennie has remembered to return there after he got into trouble. Several visions taunt Lennie as he realizes that he has done something very bad this time. George finds him there. Lennie asks George to chew him out, but George does so only half-heartedly. They discuss the farm and rabbits one last time. George tells Lennie to look across the river and see the farm. Then he shoots Lennie in the back of the head with Carlson's gun. The other men come running up and George agrees to their version of a struggle between the two men that ended in the shooting. All of the men walk back to the ranch, some sympathizing with George, others unable to decide what he's so upset about.

The Characters

Only a few characters occupy the world of *Of Mice and Men,* and most of these characters are only sketchily developed within the novel. In fact, one of the criticisms made about the book is that the characters are never fully developed but instead appear as outlines or symbols of real people. Only George and Lennie are truly memorable. The others—Candy, Crooks, Carlson, Slim, Whit, the boss, Curley, and Curley's wife—are important more as types than as individuals. They represent different aspects of the ranch's society and of American society as a whole. Candy, Crooks, and Curley's wife (to some degree) are the outcasts who face discrimination because of age, race, or sex. Carlson is selfish and heartless; Slim is quiet and understanding; Curley is aggressive and brutish.

We readers learn only a little about their histories or their present lives. They are nearly anonymous, the kinds of people George says Lennie and he have avoided becoming because of their companionship.

Why did Steinbeck depict his characters in this way? There are several possible interpretations. One is that Steinbeck, as a marine biologist, has a biological view of nature and people, rather than a people-centered one. We are a small part of nature, just part of the scenery, and not at the center of the universe. The lives of individuals are relatively unimportant in the overall scheme of things. Our life is not predetermined from the beginning but neither are we able to alter nature's grand design. George and Lennie want to change their lives, but they will never be able to change who they are.

Another explanation is that Steinbeck is developing an allegory—a moral tale—in his novelette and not presenting a story of the lives of individual people. To test this theory, as you read the book you should think about whether the characters seem alive to you or whether Steinbeck has intended them merely to be symbols within the allegory he is presenting. You should also think about what each character symbolizes. Some possible explanations are presented in the character sketches below.

You can look at the characters in still another way—not as individuals but as pairs that taken together represent two sides of an individual. It is interesting that we almost never see anyone alone during the novel; they almost always appear in twos or groups. George and Lennie are one two-sided person; Carlson and Slim another; Candy and Crooks a third. Only Curley and his wife seem to stand alone, and they are generally scorned by the others. In the following sketches, you'll have a chance to examine all of these viewpoints.

George and Lennie

The most important characters in the novel are George Milton and Lennie Small. They are ordinary workmen, moving from town to town and job to job, but they symbolize much more. Their names give us our first hints about them. One of Steinbeck's favorite books when he was growing up was *Paradise Lost* by John Milton. In this long poem, Milton describes the beginnings of evil in the world. He tells of Lucifer's fall from heaven and the creation of hell. He also describes Adam and Eve's fall from grace in the Garden of Eden. By giving George the last name of Milton, Steinbeck seems to be showing that he is an example of fallen man, someone who is doomed to loneliness and who wants to return to the Garden of Eden. Perhaps this is why George is always talking about having his own place and living "off the fat of the land," as Adam and Eve did before their fall.

Lennie is anything but small physically. He is a big man who is often described with animal images. In the opening scene of the book his hands are called paws and he snorts like a horse. Yet Lennie is small on brains and on responsibility. Someone has always taken care of Lennie and done his thinking and talking for him. First his Aunt Clara looked after him, and now George does. He is like a child, a term George uses several times in describing Lennie to Slim. Lennie has a child's short attention span and tendency to hang onto one idea stubbornly—the rabbits he will get to tend. He is innocent and "has no meanness in him."

In a sense, Lennie and George are both small men.

They will never be famous or amount to anything great. Even their dream is a modest one. The ranch George is thinking about costs only $600. They will have just a few chickens and pigs and, of course, rabbits. They won't have to work real hard.

George and Lennie are practically opposites in the way they look and in their personalities. George is described as small and quick with sharp features. Lennie is described as big, slow witted, and shapeless of face. George can comfortably fit into the ranch hands' world. He plays horseshoes with the others and goes along to the whorehouse on Saturday night. Lennie plays instead with his puppy in the barn and spends Saturday night in Crooks' room with the other outcasts—Crooks, Candy, and Curley's wife. Yet it is very difficult to look at George and Lennie separately. Over and over, under Lennie's prompting, George explains that their specialness lies in the fact that they are together. As Lennie says (repeating George's words): "But not us! An' why? Because . . . because I got you to look after me, and you got me to look after you, and that's why."

Sigmund Freud, the famous psychoanalyst, has written that each person has two sides—the *ego* and the *id*. The ego is the person's thinking side, the leader figure within him or her. The id is the physical side of the person, the body and senses. George is obviously the leader of the two men; he does all of their thinking. He remembers the things that must be remembered and instructs Lennie about them. Lennie, on the other hand, is all body. He "thinks" with his senses. The most important parts of Lennie's body are his hands. He likes to touch soft things, and he does so without thinking. That's why he keeps getting into trouble. Lennie crushes Curley's hand with his hand,

and breaks the necks of his puppy and Curley's wife when his hands get the better of him. It is interesting to note that Lennie gets in trouble only when George is not around. Steinbeck seems to be saying that a body without a mind controlling it can easily get carried away. A person must be a balance of ego and id.

Another way to look at George and Lennie is scientifically. Remember that Steinbeck was also a marine biologist. An important biological relationship is symbiosis. Many times in nature two different kinds of plants or animals live in what is called a symbiotic relationship. That means each one needs the other in order to live. George and Lennie need each other in the same way. It is obvious why Lennie needs George. George does his thinking for him and tries to keep him out of trouble. But why does George need Lennie? Lennie is more than just George's companion who keeps him from being lonely. Lennie makes George special. As George says to Slim in Chapter 3, "[Lennie] made me seem God damn smart alongside of him. . . . " He adds, "I ain't got no people. I seen the guys that go around on ranches alone. That ain't no good. They don't have no fun. After a long time they get mean." George tells Lennie that he could have so much fun without him, going into town and maybe spending his money in a whorehouse. But if he did these things he would be just like all the other nobodies on the ranch. Lennie forces George to keep repeating the vision of the future farm. George seems bored or annoyed each time he begins to tell the story, but soon he gets more excited himself. Lennie's enthusiasm keeps the vision fresh and alive. When George spots Curley's wife's body in the barn, he says, "I'll work my month an' I'll take my fifty bucks an' I'll stay all night in some lousy cat house . . . . " George knows he will be just another ranch hand without Lennie. One other way that Steinbeck hints at George's need for Lennie is that whenever George is in the bunk house without Lennie around, he plays solitaire. George is basically a loner without Lennie. So Lennie is right then when he says that George takes care of him, and he takes care of George.

There is a third way to look at the relationship of the two men—a biblical way. Remember that the Bible was also a very important influence on Steinbeck's writing. George and Lennie's story has some strong echoes of the story of Cain and Abel in Genesis. Do you remember that story? Cain draws Abel into a field and kills him. When God asks where Abel is, Cain replies, "Am I my brother's keeper?" George is not really Lennie's brother, but he is the closest thing to family that Lennie has. And George is clearly Lennie's keeper. He also is Lennie's killer. According to the Bible, after Cain kills Abel, he is forced to wander the earth alone as a fugitive, longing for Eden but never getting there. George too will be a lonely wanderer who no longer has his vision of a garden and paradise without Lennie.

Think about these possible explanations as you read the novel. Decide for yourself if you think Steinbeck is trying to look at George and Lennie's relationship in a psychological way, a biological way, a biblical way, or all three at once.

Slim and Carlson

Slim and Carlson, two of the ranch hands, make their appearances in the bunk house at almost the same time. The differences between them are striking, yet they too seem to complement each other to form a two-sided whole.

Slim is called the "prince of the ranch." He is tall, thin, and quiet. He is also almost too good to be true. His ear hears more than is said to him; he looks through and beyond people. His voice invites confidence without demanding it. He has understanding beyond thought. His actions are majestic, and he is a master craftsman. Slim is both respected and admired. Everyone seeks his approval, even Curley, who seems to have contempt for everyone else on the ranch. When Slim joins the argument in favor of killing Candy's dog, Candy knows he has to give in. Slim's word is law.

Slim is also the voice of reason and understanding. When the men discover Curley's wife's body, Slim confirms George's need to put Lennie out of his misery. He says, "An' s'pose they lock him up an' strap him down and put him in a cage. That ain't no good, George." After Lennie's killing, Slim is the only one who understands what has really happened. He consoles George and leads him away to get a drink.

Carlson presents a totally different picture of a ranch hand. His big stomach is the feature Steinbeck chooses to point out first. Carlson is coarse and insensitive. He continually illustrates his lack of concern for or understanding of other people's feelings. Carlson is the one pushing for the killing of Candy's dog. He does so not for the dog's sake, or Candy's, but because the dog's smell and looks offend his own senses. He volunteers his Luger to kill the dog and also later to use in tracking down Lennie. He even graphically demonstrates to Candy how he will shoot the old man's dog. After George has shot Lennie and is upset about it, Carlson says, "Now what the hell ya suppose is eatin' them two guys?"

Pairing Slim and Carlson will give you some interesting insights into Steinbeck's view of man within his ranch microcosm of the world. Slim is kind and perceptive. Like George, he is an "ego" figure. His majesty also makes him seem like one of the angels before the fall from heaven, as described in *Paradise Lost*. Carlson is insensitive and brutal. He is described in physical terms and, like Lennie, seems to be motivated only by his bodily senses. He is an "id" figure. He seems to symbolize a fallen angel or man.

Slim is that self-possessed man George hopes to become by owning his own place. Carlson is the type of man George wants to avoid becoming.

Taken as a pair, Slim and Carlson give us a view of man's high potential and his low reality. That Carlson's words and point of view should be the last ones Steinbeck presents in the book is an indication of the author's own sense of despair.

Candy and Crooks

Candy and Crooks are the two ultimate misfits in the novel. Each is an outcast, and each suffers discrimination. Their presence in the book provides Steinbeck with a forum for discussing his feelings about discrimination because of old age or race. Candy has a lot going against him. Not only is he old, but he is missing a hand. Hands seem to be very important in the novel (Lennie crushes Curley's hand with his hand, Curley is described as "handy" and Lennie as "not handy"), so Candy's lack of a hand shows how impotent he is. He is worried that he soon will be seen as being as useless as his dog. Then he, too, might be disposed of.

Candy plays a significant role in the novel in relation to George and Lennie's dream. By offering his life savings to help finance the farm, he brings the dream close to coming true. At the end of the book he marks the death of the dream when he suggests that he and George, without Lennie, can still get the place. George seems not even to hear what Candy has said.

Candy is the only character besides George to have a partner: his friend and longtime companion is his dog. This partnership, like George and Lennie's, is doomed to fail. There are several connections made between George and Candy and Lennie and Candy's dog. Both George and Candy state that they have no relatives. Each is upset by the prospect of being all alone, and yet each participates in the death of his partner. Candy gives his consent to Carlson to kill the dog and regrets only that he didn't shoot the dog himself. George does shoot his "dog" (Lennie), using the same gun and same method that was used for Candy's dog. Steinbeck's descriptions of the shootings of the dog and Lennie are almost parallel. Partnerships are never permanent in the world of Of Mice and Men. Steinbeck seems to be saying that laborers are always going to be lonely and rootless.

Candy also gives us a sense of what will ultimately happen to all ranch hands—they will get old and powerless and have no place to go. After all these years, Candy has just $300 to his name, and $250 of that total he received because his hand was cut off. He doesn't have any more body parts to use as insurance to protect him in his old age.

Complementing Candy in the novel and contrasting with him as well is Crooks, the black stable worker. Crooks is properly named, for his body is bent and crooked. Crooks is a proud and independent man compared to Candy. He makes a point of stating that he is not a Southern Negro, a direct descendant of slaves; his father was a California landowner. Yet Crooks too is an outcast—because of his race. Crooks is the only one of the ranch hands who has a place of his own. This "honor" may be the result of discrimination, but Crooks' pride has allowed him to turn things around. He not only doesn't seek the society of the bunk house, he also objects to Lennie and the others coming into his sanctum.

Crooks does have a big chip on his shoulder because of his racial discrimination. He reveals his anger in his attack on Lennie when the big man "invades" his room. First, Crooks challenges Lennie's right to hold onto his puppy. Then he presents a frightening vision of Lennie's life should George desert him. Yet Lennie's friendliness and innocence slowly change Crooks' attitude, and he becomes kinder toward Lennie. Even his doubts about whether the farm vision can come true slowly fade. Like Candy, Crooks asks to be part of George and Lennie's dream. He offers to work without pay in return for the companionship and independence the farm promises. All four men are misfits in the normal ranch world, and they seem to fit together. But unlike Candy, Crooks gives up on the dream. Candy still tries to get George to hold onto the vision, even after Lennie is cut off. Crooks deserts the dream when he feels George is putting him down like all the others. For Candy, a man must have a home to grow old in. To Crooks, pride is the most important thing a man can have.

What function does Crooks play in the novel? One obvious role is to give Steinbeck a way to make a statement against racial discrimination. A black man is also a necessary element if Steinbeck is attempting to create a microcosm of the larger world with his ranch community. Crooks' presence also gives us a little better understanding and respect for Lennie as a person. All the other men on the ranch look down on Crooks. "If I say something, why it's just a nigger sayin' it," he tells Lennie. But Lennie accepts Crooks as an equal, someone to "come in an' set" with. George, on the other hand, is uncomfortable that Crooks has been let in on the dream. George is not quite as liberal as we might have thought.

Curley

Curley is the only truly evil character in the book. Perhaps his name comes from the habit of villains in melodramas of the early 1900s of curling their mustaches with their fingers, or from the devil's curly tail. Or perhaps his name indicates that he is never really straight with anyone. Curley is a bully who knows he can't lose: he'll beat anyone smaller than he is, and anyone bigger who beats him will be told to pick on someone his own size.

Curley is the character most often associated with hands. Candy describes him as "handy," which in this case probably means pushy or combative. Candy also talks about Curley's keeping his hand softened with Vaseline and enclosed in a glove for his new wife's sake, a practice George finds disgusting. And Curley's hand is crushed in his fight with Lennie. Hands are also very important to Lennie, who is described as "not handy." Lennie's use of his hands is in direct contrast with Curley's. Lennie likes to feel softness with his hands; Curley's hands are filled with meanness.

Curley's inability to keep track of his wife gives us other insights into his character. He struts around like a rooster, but we know he isn't able to satisfy his wife.

He is always looking around to see if someone else is fooling with her, instead of taking care of her himself. Also, he spends Saturday night at the whorehouse with the rest of the men, and his wife seeks the company of the outcasts gathered in Crooks' room. In some ways, we can see Curley and his wife as symbols of Adam and Eve after their fall. They too have fallen far from grace.

Curley's Wife

Curley's wife is the most anonymous figure on the ranch—she doesn't even have a name. She is also perhaps the saddest figure. She married the first man who came along, and she chose badly. She wears too much makeup and shows off her body to the men in provocative ways. The man she chooses to seduce is Lennie, who has no interest in her as a woman, just as something soft. She also has a mean streak in her: she hopes Lennie will crush Curley's other hand, and she threatens to get Crooks in trouble for messing with a white woman.

It is easy to draw connections between Curley's wife and Eve. Throughout literature, women have been viewed as Eve-like, bringing evil into a man's life. Curley's wife is the direct cause of the end of George and Lennie's dream: her death marks the end of the dream. Yet she is not an evil person; she is not out to destroy herself or Lennie. Like Eve, she is just a vehicle for spreading evil.

Whit

Whit is a very minor figure in the novel. He appears only briefly and has little to say or do. His two scenes involve his discussion of a letter that a former ranch hand has sent to a magazine, and a talk with George in which he describes how the men usually spend their Saturday nights at the different whorehouses.

Whit gives undue importance to having a letter published or to choosing the right whorehouse. His purpose in the book seems to be to show us how trivial or uneventful the life of a ranch hand really is.

The Boss

The boss is another minor character. He appears briefly at the beginning to interview George and Lennie. He sets himself apart from the rest of the men on the ranch. In other words, he acts bosslike. He wears high-heeled boots and spurs to prove he is not a mere laborer. He also states his suspicions of George and Lennie traveling together. Yet we know he is not a bad guy. He did give the men a gallon of whiskey to drink on Christmas day.

Other Elements

SETTING

The action of the novel takes place on or near a ranch in the Salinas Valley of California, south of San Francisco. The time period is never stated, but it is probably during the early 1930s, the time of the Depression. The rootless wandering, poverty, and despair that George and Lennie embody are all indicative of that time.

There are three specific locations—along the banks of the Salinas River near the ranch, in the ranch bunk house, and in the barn. Just as actions in the novel follow a repeating pattern, so do the settings. The fol-

lowing act and scene breakdown of the play form of
Of Mice and Men illustrates the pattern:

ACT I
Scene 1:   Along the banks of the Salinas
              River, Thursday night
Scene 2:   The ranch bunk house, late
              the next morning

ACT II
Scene 1:   Same as Act I, Scene 2, Friday
              night
Scene 2:   In Crooks' room off the barn,
              Saturday night

ACT III
Scene 1:   Inside the barn, Sunday after-
              noon
Scene 2:   Same as Act I, Scene 1, Sun-
              day night

As you can see from the breakdown, the settings
are like a sandwich, with the riverbank location on
both edges. But while the setting at the beginning and
end is the same, the atmosphere at the spot is very
different. Everything is peaceful along the river in the
first scene; death is in the air in the last scene. These
differences are described more fully in the discussion
of the novel later in this guide.

THEMES

Steinbeck seems to have several possible themes in
mind in *Of Mice and Men*. Some of these themes are
related to the story itself and some to the idea that the
book is an allegory filled with symbolic figures rather
than a narration about real people. As you read the
book, decide which themes seem the most appropri-

ate. You should be able to back up your opinions with evidence from the book.

The American Dream

A popular theme in modern American literature is known as The American Dream. This dream involves a longing for several of the following: wealth, independence, land, good looks, popularity or fame, and self-determination. For George, the dream is to be able to have a place of his own and be his own boss. He doesn't want to work hard or make a lot of money, just enough to be free to run his own life. For Lennie, the dream is to have a piece of responsibility, the rabbits he will tend, and a sense of self-worth. Candy is looking for security in his old age and a feeling of belonging somewhere. Crooks is looking for the self-respect he felt his father had when he was a landowner. Curley's wife is looking "to make something of herself," to have nice clothes, and to have pictures taken of her.

The American Dream is almost never achieved. Even the rich and famous, such as the characters in F. Scott Fitzgerald's novel *The Great Gatsby*, find that their lives are shallow. And the working-class people, such as Biff and Willy Loman in Arthur Miller's play *Death of a Salesman*, end up disillusioned or destroy themselves. George and Lennie have a lot in common with the Lomans. They try to deny their small place in the world, but their American Dream is always a month and a hundred dollars away.

Loneliness

Loneliness and rootlessness haunt the characters in *Of Mice and Men*. Steinbeck seems to be saying that "the little man" is doomed to a life of isolation and cannot change his status. Nearly everyone in the book is a loner, and all are suspicious of George and Lennie's companionship. What creates this loneliness? Poverty is one element. Only Candy seems to have any money in the bank, and his savings are the result of losing his hand. Discrimination because of old age, race, or sex also isolates several of the characters. And the lack of a true home also creates loneliness for many of them.

Steinbeck presents several symbols of this loneliness. George continually plays solitaire when Lennie isn't around. Curley's wife keeps wandering around the ranch, and Curley is always one step behind as he searches for her. Candy's dog is taken from him and killed. Crooks lives in an isolated shack. Most of the characters seem to feel out of place wherever they are.

The Common Man

Steinbeck's focus in *Of Mice and Men* is on a group of relatively unimportant people. And the author never tries to make them seem more important than they are. They are just common men who will always be fairly anonymous and powerless. The title of the book is not even taken from the Bible or another major work. It comes from a short poem by Robert Burns with the long title, "To a Mouse On Turning Her Up in Her Nest with a Plow, November, 1785." According to the poem: "The best laid schemes o' mice and men/Gang aft a-gley [often go astray],/And lea'e us nought but grief and pain,/For promised joy." Steinbeck is sensitive to the needs and feelings of the common people in the novel, but he is not hopeful for the success of their "best laid schemes."

Naturalism or Realism

Closely related to the common man theme is Steinbeck's creation of a naturalistic or realistic atmosphere. Steinbeck is not a romantic who makes a big deal about people or natural wonders. Like a scientist, he observes things as they are and sees people as just a small part of the overall natural world.

A Political Statement

Some readers wonder if Steinbeck is trying to make a political statement in the novel. Is he attacking the forces that have doomed the characters to their sad lives? This argument doesn't seem to hold up well. No highly placed figures are attacked in the book. The only leader is the boss, and he is pictured as a basically nice guy. Even in his more political books—*The Grapes of Wrath*, about migrant workers, and *In Dubious Battle*, about unions and strikes—Steinbeck never seems to be creating propaganda or calling for an overthrow of the system. Steinbeck is more of an observer than a rabble-rouser. The feeling the reader gets is sadness rather than anger.

The Search for the Holy Grail

One of Steinbeck's favorite books was *Le Morte d'Arthur*, Sir Thomas Malory's retelling of the stories of King Arthur and the Knights of the Round Table, and the King Arthur legends play a part in several of Steinbeck's works. One of those legends was Sir Galahad's search for the Holy Grail, the cup from which Jesus was said to have drunk. Finding the Grail will cause all sins to be forgiven, according to the knights. Throughout literature, the Grail serves as a symbol of that which is sought but can never be possessed. Galahad was the only knight pure enough to find and touch the Grail, but once he touched it, he died and his spirit went to heaven.

George and Lennie's search for a place to live off the fat of the land is a kind of search for the Grail. And, like true Knights of the Round Table, they possess such qualities as loyalty and the creation of a bond between them. But no one but Sir Galahad ever succeeded in this quest. Coincidentally, many of the others found their relationships and quests destroyed by a woman, just as George and Lennie do.

The Story of Cain and Abel

The connections between George and Lennie and Cain and Abel of Genesis have already been discussed in The Characters section of this guide. One important critic, Peter Lisca, has pointed out some other interesting parallels between the two stories. Lisca notes that many of the characters' names in *Of Mice and Men* start with the letter C—Curley, Candy, Crooks, Curley's wife. They are all descendants of Cain, people doomed to live in isolation in a fallen world. No character's name starts with *A* because there were no descendants of Abel.

STYLE

Steinbeck's style in the novel is conversational and direct. People are talking throughout most of the book. They talk in the natural language of the ranch—lots of cursing, name calling, and slang. The style fits in well with the common man and naturalistic themes you just read about.

While Steinbeck's language and style are natural and simple, his sentences are carefully constructed.

His descriptions are almost like poetry. Here is a sentence from the first paragraph of the book: "The water is warm too, for it has slipped twinkling over the yellow sands in the sunlight before reaching the narrow pool." Notice how the author has repeated *w* sounds in the first clause and *s* sounds in the second. This is called alliteration. You might look for other examples of alliteration in the first few pages, and throughout the book. Steinbeck also uses similes to create pictures in the reader's mind: the rabbits sit on the bank "like gray, sculptured stones," and Lennie snorts into the water "like a horse."

Another aspect of Steinbeck's style is that he lets the story develop one step at a time; he doesn't jump ahead or flash back. This gives the action a dramatic quality. We know Lennie has a potential for violence, so we are a little afraid when he confronts Curley in the bunk house or begins petting Curley's wife's hair in the barn. But Steinbeck lets each of these scenes start off slowly then build quickly to a powerful climax. We, as readers, get caught up in the drama because of the way he presents the scenes to us.

POINT OF VIEW

Of Mice and Men is told from an objective, third-person point of view. Since the book is really a play in novel form (see the Form and Structure section, pages 29–30), we get to see the characters reveal themselves slowly through their dialogue. Only late in the book do we begin to realize that some events have been foreshadowed, or hinted at, by earlier happenings. In a sense, Steinbeck allows us to observe the action from our own point of view and develop our own opinions about the characters.

FORM AND STRUCTURE

In his letters, Steinbeck wrote that he planned to try out a new form with *Of Mice and Men*. He called this form a play-novelette, that is, the novel would be a lot like a play. There should be a lot of dialogue, not a lot of description, and the action should take place in only a few locations.

Each chapter of the book is like a scene from a play. It opens with a description of the setting. Then the action is presented mostly through dialogue and builds to a dramatic moment or a calm resolution, followed by the curtain's coming down. You can therefore look at each chapter as a separate piece in which the action starts slowly, builds, and then falls (quickly or slowly). You might want to look for this pattern within each chapter as you read and even draw a diagram to trace the rising and falling movements of events in each scene. Then notice how the events follow similar patterns in later scenes.

The repeating pattern of events is part of another technique, called foreshadowing. Foreshadowing involves having early events in a book hint at later events. For example, the death of Candy's dog foreshadows Lennie's death. They are shot with the same gun in the same way. And Candy's comment that a man shouldn't let a stranger shoot his dog gives us an understanding of why George knows he must shoot Lennie himself.

Steinbeck's use of foreshadowing is at times obvious, and some readers think he overworks the technique. As you read the novel, you might think about how effective Steinbeck's foreshadowing is as a device for keeping the story moving along. You should also decide if the technique increases your appreciation of

Steinbeck's skill as a writer or if it makes what happens later on seem too obvious.

The structure of the novel also follows a circular pattern. This was pointed out in the discussion of the book's settings a few pages ago. The book opens and closes in the same location. The changes in the description of that setting show us just how much has changed in the lives of George and Lennie since the beginning of the story.

The Story

The story line of *Of Mice and Men* seems on the surface to be pretty simple and ordinary. Steinbeck did that on purpose. He wanted to show a world of ordinary people, primarily working-class men, living their day-to-day lives within a normal world. Events follow one another in a fairly natural, unemotional pattern. In fact, Steinbeck had originally planned to call his novel *Something that Happened*.

Yet during the book's "calm" three-day period, lots of unusual "somethings" happen. You'll read about such extraordinary events as the murder of two people, the killing of two animals, an attempted seduction, a fight that results in the crushing of a man's hand, discrimination against two ranch hands because of race and old age, the destruction of a life-long friendship, and the evaporation of a dream.

So, one thing is clear: don't be fooled by the simplicity of the novel. It is often true in literature that a plain surface hides a complex core. You're going to have to stay alert as you read and keep in mind what

each character says and does. Also, pay close attention to the setting descriptions at the start of each
chapter. All of these will be important, as you'll see
below.

Steinbeck's story line is very tightly constructed.
The various incidents are closely interrelated. In many
ways, the events described in the novel follow a circular pattern. That is, an event that occurs early in the
book will often be echoed by an event that occurs later
on. For example, both the first scene of the book and
the last one take place on the banks of the Salinas
River. And some aspects of the conclusion are hinted
at in the opening scene.

This technique of placing hints throughout a story
is called *foreshadowing*, discussed earlier in the Form
and Structure section. You'll also learn more about
Steinbeck's use of foreshadowing in the discussion of
Chapter 3, pages 45–52.

Here is one other thing to think about as you read
the novel: Steinbeck has intended the book to be an
allegory, a story in which the events and characters
are symbols and in which a moral is implied. You'll
learn more about Steinbeck's use of symbolism in the
novel in the chapter-by-chapter discussion below.

Now that you have a little greater understanding of
Steinbeck's motives and style, it's time to begin look-
ing more closely at the story line of *Of Mice and
Men*.

CHAPTER 1: AT THE RIVER

The book opens along the banks of the Salinas River
a few miles south of Soledad, California. Everything is
calm and beautiful, and nature is alive. The trees are
green and fresh, lizards are skittering along, rabbits sit
on the sand. There are no people in the scene.

Notice the words and images that Steinbeck uses in the description. His writing is filled with such devices as alliteration, repetition of words, similes, and metaphors. (You read about these language elements in the Style section of this guide.)

As Steinbeck's "word camera" pans along the scene, it stops to focus on the first indication of the presence of people—a worn path. The path has been "beaten hard" and is littered with an ash pile. These images tell us something about the mark men have made on this natural setting: they have left destruction (ashes and barkless limbs) in their wake.

Suddenly, the calm is broken. Trouble is in the air. Animals begin to scatter. Two men have arrived on the scene, and the environment seems troubled by their presence. A heron near the river flees from the scene, but it doesn't move gracefully. Instead, Steinbeck uses harsh words such as "labored" and "pounded" to describe its flight from the river. For a moment the scene becomes "lifeless." Then in walk George and Lennie.

From their first description, George and Lennie are opposites. George is small and quick, with clearly defined features. He is obviously the "brains" of the pair. Lennie, on the other hand, is huge and shapeless. He is not so much a man as a human animal.

Look over this first description of Lennie to see how often Steinbeck uses animal images to describe him. Lennie is at once a bear and a horse. He has paws instead of hands, and drinks water as a snorting horse does. Contrast Lennie's approach to the river with George's. George is cautious and aloof. We as readers don't know it yet, but this river will be a part of another very important scene at the end of the book. The attitudes of the two men toward the water—Lennie's trust and George's caution—will be reflected at that time as well.

NOTE: Lennie and Animal Imagery   One of the issues of the book is how human Lennie really is and whether he is capable of living in a human world. Look out for comparisons of Lennie with animals as you read and decide what insights they give you into Lennie's character and Steinbeck's style.

With the scene now set with these stage directions, the characters begin their dialogue. George's first words are sharp and critical of Lennie, while Lennie's response is innocent and generous: "Tha's good," he says. "You drink some, George. You take a good big drink." George does drink but is careful to warn Lennie of the hazards of bad water.

You are probably wondering what the relationship is between these two men. There are a lot of different possibilities. Are they brothers? Father and son? Friends? Can they really be friends if they are such complete opposites? What forces have brought them together and are keeping them together? You will get some of the answers in Chapter 1 and more in Chapter 2. George and Lennie are traveling companions, but they are a lot like family. George promised Lennie's Aunt Clara, who is now dead, that he would look after Lennie. As we discover, they really look after each other. George takes care of Lennie's physical needs, and Lennie helps George fill his emotional needs, such as the need to be responsible and caring for another person.

The dialogue continues to follow this pattern of critical comments from George and innocent responses from Lennie through the next several pages. George's ranting seems to have little effect on Lennie. He has obviously heard it all before, or he is just too stupid to recognize George's sarcasm. George's emotions run from impatient to angry to exasperated, while Lennie's move swiftly back and forth between sad and happy.

Little by little, we discover that the two men have been traveling together for some time. Two elements make this clear. One is Lennie's constant imitation of George's actions. He acts like George's dog or younger brother. He obviously trusts George in a way that could come only from long association with him. A second element is George's knowing exactly what Lennie is doing, even when Lennie is trying to be secretive. When George sees Lennie's hand sneak into his pocket, he immediately asks, "What'd you take outa that pocket?" He demands to see Lennie's "treasure"—a dead mouse. And after George has thrown the mouse across the river, he knows that Lennie has gone to retrieve it.

NOTE: The Title   The mouse that George and Lennie throw around is not the reason for the book's title. The title is taken from a poem by Robert Burns that includes the lines "The best laid schemes o' mice and men/Gang aft a-gley," or often go astray. As you will see, George and Lennie have big plans, but the title gives a good hint that things may not turn out too well. The title may also relate to the two sides of Lennie—the person and animal. Or it may relate to the famous expression, "Are you a man or a mouse?" The expression means, are you brave or cowardly? There are lots of cowards in the novel, but not too many brave people.

After George has thrown the mouse away a second time, the relationship of the two men comes into clearer focus. Lennie starts to "blubber like a baby," and George begins to comfort him. "I ain't takin' it away jus' for meanness," George says. "That mouse ain't fresh, Lennie; and besides, you've broke it pettin' it. You get another mouse that's fresh and I'll let you keep it a little while." George obviously cares for Lennie a great deal. And Lennie is obviously a mixture of little kid and crazy adult. George is the thinker, the brains and the mouth of their partnership. He tells Lennie "not to say nothin' " when they see their new boss on the ranch. Lennie is the strength of the pair. His hands are his most important feature. His sense of touch is one he uses most. He prefers even a rotting dead mouse to a rubber one that "wasn't no good to pet." George, with his eyes and brains, spots the wood they will need for their campfire, but Lennie gathers the wood.

Their conversation has also touched on a troubling event, one that foreshadows an even more tragic happening later in the story. The two of them had to run from their last town, Weed, because of something that Lennie did that he has already forgotten about. The event involved "some girls coming by." Exactly what happened is not yet revealed, but you shouldn't let mysterious references such as these slip by unnoticed. They usually have lots of hidden meaning. We learn a little more about the incident a few pages later. Lennie was just feeling a girl's dress when she began to yell, and the two men had to hide and run away. Now they are moving on to a new town and new jobs.

But they are not heading straight to the ranch where they will be working. Instead, they are spending their last night of freedom in the woods. Lennie is concerned about what they will eat, but George's thoughts are on being a free man for one more day.

George begins another attack on Lennie, declaring that without the burden of looking after Lennie he could "live so easy." He could get a job, earn his money, and spend it on whiskey and a cathouse. Then why does George stay with Lennie? Because their relationship makes the two of them special.

Under Lennie's prompting George articulates the specialness of the two of them. He begins his declaration in rhythmic tones, "as though he has said [the words] many times before":

> Guys like us, that work on ranches, are the lone-liest guys in the world. They got no family. They don't belong no place. They come to a ranch an' work up a stake and then they go inta town and blow their stake, and the first thing you know they're poundin' their tail on some other ranch. They ain't got nothing to look ahead to.

But Lennie's excitement at hearing the words and his interjections cause George to change his tone of voice. Little by little, his excitement builds too as he describes the farm they will have and the animals Lennie will get to tend. The words are no longer just oft-repeated words; they have become almost a litany, a kind of prayer. Are you getting caught up in the excitement? Steinbeck wants you to be. He will be working on your emotions throughout the book.

What George is describing is often labeled "The American Dream." This dream involves the desire to have material possessions and the independence that being free from needing things can give you. Most characters in modern American literature are seeking this dream, but few ever achieve it. (The American

Dream was defined in the Themes section of this guide.)

Now that Lennie has gotten George into a good mood, Lennie takes the upper hand in the relationship and begins to press it. He threatens to run away if George continues to pick on him. George quickly gives in, and we know his anger with Lennie isn't real. Lennie needs George to look after him, but George needs Lennie just as much. Lennie makes George understand his specialness and keeps the dream alive. These points are dealt with more fully in the discussion of Chapter 3 and earlier in The Characters section of this guide.

The chapter closes with the two men going to sleep around the dying embers of their campfire. Lennie presses once more about the rabbits he will get to tend and threatens to leave one more time. George tells him to "go to hell" with one final moment of mock anger. Everything is peaceful again. The only sounds are those of nature, alive again as it was at the beginning before the two men arrived. One small circle has been completed.

CHAPTER 2: IN THE BUNK HOUSE

The next morning George and Lennie arrive at the ranch where they will work. From the first we know that this ranch is not one of the rich spreads that we have often seen on television. This ranch is poor, like George and Lennie and like American society as a whole in the early 1930s.

NOTE: The Ranch as a Microcosm   Steinbeck has said that he intended the ranch in *Of Mice and Men* to be a microcosm of American society. A microcosm is a miniature world. Individual people within a microcosm represent groups of people in the larger world. The ranch has many of the qualities of the rural U.S. during the Depression—poverty, loneliness, a homeless feeling. See if you can spot these qualities in some of the stories told about ranch life in this chapter, particularly those of Candy and Whit. The people on the ranch also represent many of the different kinds of people who lived in rural California and throughout this country during the 1930s. You will meet all of the different characters in this chapter. As you do, think about them two ways—as individual people and as symbols of groups in American society.

The second chapter, like the first, opens with a setting description. This one sounds like stage directions for a play. Steinbeck carefully takes us through the one-room bunk house. He points out even minor details, such as what type of boxes are nailed over each bunk and exactly what items are to be found stored in the boxes.

Do you notice a difference in style between the openings of Chapter 1 and Chapter 2? Look at Steinbeck's sentence structure and even his choice of words. Which opener seems more interesting or gives you a more positive feeling about the world? Remember that Steinbeck's description of nature at the beginning of Chapter 1 was filled with imagery and interesting language patterns. The sentences were long and smooth flowing, like the river. The sentences in the bunk house description are short and bare, just like the room itself. Compare the first two sentences in each chapter:

> A few miles south of Soledad, the Salinas River drops in close to the hillside bank and runs deep and green. The water is warm too, for it has slipped twinkling over the yellow sands in the sunlight before reaching the narrow pool.
>
> The bunk house was a long, rectangular building. Inside, the walls were whitewashed and the floor unpainted.

Steinbeck has taken us from the world of nature to the world of civilization. How do you think he wants us to feel about this change? It is clear that the author doesn't seem too thrilled about it. We can tell this by the series of events and descriptions that follow.

The first person who greets George and Lennie and introduces us to ranch life is not a handsome cowboy; he is a stoop-shouldered old man carrying a broom. Candy informs the two men that they are already in hot water with the boss. He's "sore as hell" because they didn't arrive in time for the morning work shift. Candy points out their bunks with his handless right arm. Candy seems like something out of a Halloween story.

George immediately notices a problem with the bunk. The person who had the bunk last has left behind a can of roach powder. The powder will kill various insects that George refers to as "pants rabbits." Why does he choose the word "rabbit" here? It stands out because of Lennie's passion for rabbits that we learned about in the first scene. One interpretation might be to contrast nature in the outside world with nature in the bunk house. Rabbits outside are soft and promise good things; pants rabbits inside are "scourges." Or maybe Steinbeck wants to show us a contrast between Lennie's gentle, soft view of nature and George's more sarcastic view.

Candy quickly begins to defend his bunk house world by pointing out that the guy who used that bunk was a neatness freak. He washed his hands even *after* he ate. George is still not convinced and wants to know why the man quit. "Why . . . . he . . . . just quit, the way a guy will," Candy says. People move around a lot in the ranch world. Nothing stays permanently, except maybe the bugs.

George lifts his mattress and Lennie imitates him. This is the first time Lennie has been mentioned in the chapter. He is clearly following George's instructions about not standing out.

Candy continues with his description of the people on the ranch. He mentions Crooks and the boss, the two opposite extremes of the ranch society. Crooks is the black stable buck who handles the dirty work around the ranch. Candy is fascinated by Crooks, who is both a "nigger" and reads a lot. We will learn more about Crooks in Chapter 4.

George is more interested in the boss, the other end of the scale. Candy tells him the boss has a temper but is pretty nice. He even gave the men a whole gallon of whiskey on Christmas Day. On that day Crooks was allowed to enter the main bunk house, only to be pushed into a fight. Following the fight the men, except for Candy (too old) and Crooks (black), headed into town to a whorehouse. Why do you think Steinbeck mentions this strange Christmas celebration? He could be trying to show how informal or simple the ranch world is. He could be trying to illustrate examples of discrimination in the society. Or he could be trying to help us understand Candy's character a little more by showing us the kinds of things he thinks about.

The boss arrives. He doesn't enter, he just stands in

the doorway in a bosslike stance. His thumbs are stuck in his belt and he is wearing high-heeled boots that distinguish him from the workers. Candy notices the boss and immediately changes from a talkative guide to a quiet servant. He rubs his whiskers and shuffles from the room. The changes in Candy are another indication of how the ranch reflects the class structure of American society as a whole. It is a microcosm.

The boss begins to question George and Lennie about their late arrival. He then asks their names. For the first time, we learn their last names—Milton and Small. This is also our first indication that the book may be a symbolic story, an *allegory*.

NOTE: The Story as Allegory . An allegory is a common literary device. It is usually a short story or book that tries to get across an important message about how people live or how they should live. Characters in an allegory usually stand for ideas and their names often show the ideas they stand for. When you see names in a story that sound like symbols, you should ask yourself, What messages is this author trying to get across here? Suggestions of what George and Lennie's names might stand for are in The Characters section of this guide. Think about the other characters' names as well. Most of them are short and descriptive—Crooks, Curley, Slim, the boss, Candy. They sound more like nicknames than names. Crooks' and Curley's names may show us that the ranch society isn't as straight or strong as it might be. Slim is the only really strong person on the ranch, but his name indicates that the ranch life is "slim" on strength as well.

The boss continues to question the new men, and George answers all the questions. He doesn't want Lennie's dumbness to show and maybe cost them their jobs. When Lennie does say something, two things happen—George scowls at him and the boss begins to address Lennie. Lennie starts to panic, as he often does when he's put on the spot. To ease the boss' suspicions, George begins to make up a story about why he and Lennie travel around together.

George often has to defend his staying with Lennie. Why can't he just tell people that they like each other and enjoy sticking together? Maybe it's because he is a little ashamed of traveling with a dummy like Lennie. But if that were true, why have they stuck together so long? Perhaps it is because he is uncomfortable admitting that he gets lonely. Loneliness is a part of life on this ranch and in our world. Nobody likes it, but we have all learned to live with it. As Candy says, "A guy on a ranch don't never listen nor he don't ast no questions." As we will see later on, the ones who are bothered the most by loneliness—Candy, Crooks, and Curley's wife—all try to link themselves with the dream vision that George and Lennie present.

After the boss leaves, George gets mad at Lennie for forgetting not to say anything. He notices that Candy has been listening, and yells at him for being nosy. Then he notices Candy's old dog. Keep your eye on this dog. He will play a big role in the story, foreshadowing future events.

A new character enters the bunk house, the boss' son Curley, who wears high-heeled boots like his father. Curley is always looking for someone. This time he is looking for his father; often he will be looking for his wife. Whenever Curley shows up he makes people feel uncomfortable. He is always trying to start a fight. You probably know people like Curley, and dislike them. They bring out the worst in everyone they meet.

Curley immediately starts to take on Lennie. He seems always to go after someone he thinks is weaker than he is. In the next two pages we are shown contrasts between Curley and Lennie. Curley is a "lightweight, and he's handy." He's a small man who picks fights. Lennie is big and "not handy." George warns that Lennie doesn't like to fight, but he usually wins because he "don't know no rules." This last remark seems to be another comparison of Lennie with animals.

Why do you think Steinbeck is telling us all these things? One reason is probably to get us to like Lennie, because he's an underdog being picked on by a bully, and to dislike Curley. Another reason may be to warn us through foreshadowing that there is potential danger for Lennie and for George and Lennie's togetherness on this ranch. George senses this danger and says, "Look, Lennie! This here ain't no set up. I'm scared." George even repeats his instructions to Lennie to return to the riverbank if there should be any big trouble.

Another dangerous person, Curley's wife, comes into the room next. She's wearing lots of makeup and flashy clothes. She stands in the doorway showing off her body to the new men. Lennie is fascinated by her, but George is angry. George and Candy agree that she's a "tart." Once again, George has to warn Lennie about the potential danger he spots.

You're probably beginning to get worried for Lennie by now. He seems so innocent, like a little child, and he's vulnerable too. Can he really survive all of these dangers? Lennie doesn't think so. He says, "I don' like this place, George. This ain't no good place. I wanna get outa here." George reluctantly says they've got to stay for a little while. They've got to get a little bit of a stake together to help pay for their dream farm. Little by little the hopefulness we and the characters felt at the end of the first chapter is starting to wear away.

The last two important characters enter the bunk house. They are Slim and Carlson. Throughout the book these two men will present us with opposite views of ranch life and ranch people. (You read more about them and what they symbolize in The Characters section of this guide.)

Slim is the "prince" of the ranch. He is like a Greek god or knight of the Round Table. He's almost not human. What would you think of someone whose word was always accepted as law, whose "ear heard more than was said to him," and who had "understanding beyond thought"? Slim seems too good to be true, doesn't he? George is willing to tell him his true feelings about Lennie: "It's a lot nicer to go around with a guy you know," he says. He will discuss their relationship more fully with Slim in the next chapter.

Carlson is a lot more "earthy" than Slim. The first thing we learn about him is that he has a pot belly. He makes a joke on Lennie's name, and then proceeds to ask about Slim's "bitch." At first we think Carlson is swearing, but we learn that Slim has a female dog who has given birth to puppies. Both Carlson and Lennie want one of those puppies. Lennie wants one to pet; Carlson wants one to replace Candy's old dog, which he wants to have shot.

Slim and Carlson show us two opposite sets of qualities. Slim presents good will, compassion, and understanding. Carlson presents a lack of concern for others' feelings. We'll see more of these two men and their qualities in later chapters.

As the chapter draws to a close, George agrees to ask Slim for a puppy for Lennie and also nearly starts to fight with Curley. We see a mix of love and fear. Are things hopeful or not? We'll soon see.

CHAPTER 3: VIOLENCE ERUPTS

As Chapter 3 opens we are still in the bunk house later the same day. The men have finished working for the day, and there is a calmness in the air.

This scene also opens with a description of the setting. This time the description involves images of light and darkness next to each other. Outside there is "evening brightness," inside there is "dusk." Slim and George enter the dark bunk house together and turn on a "brilliant" light. You have already seen in the first two chapters that the opening description of the setting helps to create an atmosphere for the whole chapter, so you probably suspect that this chapter will deal with opposites. Some of the events will be "dark" and upsetting and some will be "bright" and promising. If that's your feeling, you're right.

George and Slim continue the conversation they began in the last chapter. Once again George is willing to open up his true feelings to Slim. For the first time we learn all the facts about the history of Lennie and George's partnership. Lennie has always been retarded. He was brought up by his Aunt Clara, and when she died Lennie began going places with George. At first George took advantage of Lennie's stupidity and innocence. But when he realized that

Lennie would do anything he said, even something dangerous, George stopped kidding him.

Little by little, George has come to realize what Lennie means to him. Lennie makes George feel "God damn smart alongside him." He also helps him avoid the loneliness that is "no fun" and causes a ranch hand to "get mean." Slim understands all of this and supports George's opinions fully.

George feels so secure talking to Slim that he even reveals what happened in Weed that caused George and Lennie to flee. Lennie, with his passion for soft things, began feeling a girl's soft dress. She screamed, Lennie panicked and tore the dress, the girl accused him of rape, and a posse chased after the men. They hid in an irrigation ditch. Water seems always to provide George and Lennie with safety.

Remember this story. In fact, remember all of the events that occur in this chapter. They are part of Steinbeck's foreshadowing technique.

NOTE: Steinbeck's Use of Foreshadowing   Foreshadowing is a writing technique that involves having early events or descriptions in a story give hints about what will happen later. You've probably seen this technique used a lot in mystery stories you have read or seen on television. For example, the wind begins to whistle and a dog howls. Later the hero discovers that a murder occurred at exactly that time. Or a victim reads about a gruesome death in a book and is later killed in just that way. Foreshadowing is used to build drama or suspense.

Steinbeck uses foreshadowing often in his books, particularly in *Of Mice and Men*. It is one of the main ways that he moves that story along and links one event to another. Watch for the following events in this chapter: the description of the "rape" in Weed, the killing of Candy's dog and Candy's response to it, and Lennie's fight with Curley. Each will be echoed in later parts of the book. All of these events involve violence, so there is sure to be more violence to come.

You can read more about Steinbeck's use of foreshadowing in the section of this guide entitled Form and Structure.

While George continues his conversation with Slim, Lennie walks into the bunk house. He is crouched over. George knows exactly what is going on. Lennie is hiding his puppy just as he had hidden the mouse the night before. George warns him, prophetically, that he'll kill the puppy if he handles it too much.

The rest of the men come into the bunk house after their game of horseshoes. When Carlson enters, Steinbeck presents another pair of light/dark images. Carlson turns on a light and declares "Darker'n hell in here." This line is setting us up for what is to come next—a dark moment.

Carlson begins pressuring Candy to shoot his dog. He says it's for the dog's own good, but that's not true. Carlson's senses are offended by the dog's smell and the fact that "he don't have no fun." Slim tells Candy, "I wisht somebody'd shoot me if I get old an' a cripple." Since Candy is the only old cripple on the ranch, he is probably a little worried by this last comment.

Why do you think Carlson wants to get rid of the dog so badly? And why does Steinbeck present such a long scene around the killing of the dog? Here are a few possible reasons. Decide which one or ones you think may be right.

For one thing, Steinbeck wants to show that Carlson and the other ranch hands live only for today. They can't understand why Candy would prefer an old, crippled dog to a new puppy. Ranch hands like Carlson, don't think about the past or the future. They work for a month, spend their money on Saturday night fun, and start over again from scratch. Maybe that's why most of them have trouble understanding why George and Lennie want to plan for the future. Candy's dog is part of his past and a symbol of future old age of all of the men. Carlson wants to remove this reminder.

Here's a second possible reason. All of the ranch hands are loners, except George and Lennie, and Candy with his dog. Killing the dog restores nearly total loneliness to the bunk house world.

A third reason may be that Carlson wants to show his manhood by killing the dog. When Candy challenges Carlson about whether he has a gun, Carlson says proudly, "The hell I ain't. Got a luger." He then puts the pistol in his hip pocket like some Western gunslinger. Steinbeck may be showing us how far this "new West" has fallen from the "old West" of movie, book, and magazine fame. Carlson is not out to kill an outlaw to prove his manhood. He's going to shoot an old, crippled animal.

Still a fourth reason involves Steinbeck's foreshadowing technique. We'll learn more about what is being foreshadowed later.

Whatever the reason, Candy eventually does give in, largely because Slim backs Carlson, and Slim's word is law. Carlson continues to demonstrate his lack of compassion before and after the shooting. He shows Candy exactly how he will shoot the dog and then afterwards cleans his gun in front of Candy.

Meanwhile, a new character has come into the bunkhouse—Whit. Whit makes only two brief appearances in the book, both during this chapter. In one appearance he reads a letter written by one of the former ranch hands to a popular western magazine. In the other appearance he tells George about the way to spend a Saturday night in town, in the right whorehouse.

What is Whit's role in the book? He seems to have two. One, he shows us what the life of a ranch hand is like when he is not working. He reads cheap magazines and spends his money on Saturday night entertainment. Whit's excitement in describing both pastimes tells us a little about the emptiness of ranch life.

Whit's second role is to take our minds off of the killing of the dog. Through Whit, Steinbeck seems to be saying that death is a natural part of life, even if man causes it. He doesn't want us to feel too emotional about the event.

Meanwhile, a more interesting situation is developing. Curley has come into the bunk house looking once again for his wife. He suspects that she may be in the barn with Slim, and is going looking for him. You've probably seen situations like this before. Someone is out to pick a fight, and everyone wants to go watch it. All of the men rush out, except for George, Lennie, and Candy.

George and Lennie start talking. George warns Lennie to stay away from Curley's wife. All women are trouble, he says, and the only safe woman is a whore. Since we're getting used to Steinbeck's foreshadowing, we're starting to suspect that warnings like these are to be taken seriously. They are hints of bad things to come.

Lennie is getting a little worried too and asks George to reassure him about the dream farm again. George starts off without hesitating this time. This version of the dream is similar to the one we heard last night, but it is not exactly the same. Everything seems even more real now. George even names the kind of trees and crops they will plant, the kinds of animals they will have, and the kind of house they will live in. The vision sounds so real that Candy, who is listening, asks George, "You know where's a place like that?" It turns out that George does indeed have a real place in mind. The ranch costs only $600, but it might as well cost $6000 as far as George and Lennie are concerned. They don't have any money. Candy offers to put up more than half of the money. He has $300 in the bank, most of it received when his hand was cut off. He even agrees to leave his share to the other two men when he dies. All Candy wants is security in his old age and a place of his own for a little while.

Remember the discussion about light and dark images at the beginning of this scene? Good feelings (light) now seem to have replaced the dark clouds caused by the killing of the dog. Steinbeck comments, "This thing they had never really believed in was coming true." Both George and Lennie experience unusual religious feelings. In a "reverent" way, George says, "Jesus Christ! I bet we could swing her," and Lennie adds, in his imitating way, "I bet by Christ he [the puppy] likes it there, by Jesus."

Why do you think Candy is the one who wants to be part of the dream instead of one of the other men, such as Slim or Whit? Maybe because Candy is as afraid of loneliness as George and Lennie. Or maybe because he feels as out of place in the bunk house as they do. Or maybe because he is the only other person on the ranch who understands the importance of companionship.

Now that Candy is accepted as a friend, he can confide a deeply important and personal thought to George. He tells George that he should have shot his dog himself and not let a stranger do it. Remember his comment: it's another important moment of foreshadowing.

We have now seen one dark event and one light event in this chapter. We're about to confront another dark happening. Curley, who did not fight Slim, comes into the bunk house. He is still itching for a fight. When he sees Lennie still smiling over the thought of the future ranch, Curley thinks Lennie is smirking at him. He begins to punch the big man and draws blood. Lennie doesn't know what to do until George urges him to fight back. He grabs Curley's hand in his "paw" and flops the man around until the hand is crushed.

NOTE: Hand Images   In the fight between Curley and Lennie, we are swamped with mentions of the word "hand" or with hand images. In fact, "hand" or its synonyms are used more than 100 times in the novel. Curley is "handy"; Lennie is "not handy"; Lennie has paws; Candy is missing a hand. Steinbeck seems to be trying to show us that the people on the ranch are manual laborers, people who use their hands more than, or instead of, their brains. Slim's comment to Curley after the fight seems to fit this idea. Slim asks Curley, whose hand is crushed, "You got your senses in hand enough to listen?" Look for more hand images in the book and remember that it is Lennie's thinking and acting with his hands that usually gets him in trouble.

The scene draws to a close with Slim's convincing Curley to say his hand got caught in a machine and George's assuring Lennie that he did nothing wrong. Violence is a natural part of the ranch world, as it is in nature. Once again everything is calm as the curtain falls on another scene.

CHAPTER 4: THE OUTCASTS

You have probably noticed that until the fight at the end of Chapter 3, George and not Lennie has been in the center of the action and a part of the conversations going on at the ranch. That's all going to change. The focus is shifting now, and Lennie is going to be taking over throughout most of the rest of the book. And from what we've already seen of Lennie, we can guess that bad things are likely to happen.

One way that Steinbeck signals that changing focus is to move the setting of Chapter 4 from the bunk house to a place outside of the main life of the ranch. Steinbeck chooses as his "outside" setting Crooks' room off of the barn. Interestingly enough, there will be several more setting changes before the end of the book, but the action will never return to the bunk house. Things will never get back to normal. This switch of setting as a way to change the focus from George to Lennie makes sense because, as we have seen, George can fit into the bunk house life, but Lennie can't. George plays horseshoes with the other men and goes along to the whorehouse. Meanwhile, Lennie stays in the barn to play with his puppy.

Choosing the black man's room as the setting makes sense for another reason. Steinbeck wants us to feel the isolation and discrimination that misfits such as Lennie, Candy, Crooks, and Curley's wife have to deal with. As we discover early in the chapter, only the boss and Slim have ever entered Crooks' room. Crooks is isolated both by his skin color and by the home he has been assigned.

You've all seen cluttered rooms, but not many have as much stuff in them as Crooks' room. Part of the stuff is for Crooks himself and part of it is for the horses. Steinbeck describes all of the possessions in detail. Crooks has a lot of things, but look carefully at them. There are broken harnesses and split collars and drippy cans of tar. Nothing is whole. Even Crooks' personal items include tattered books, battered magazines, and gold-rimmed glasses hanging from a nail. Remember the description of the bunk house at the beginning of the last chapter? Compare this room with that one. There are several contrasts you could make, particularly about openness and closeness and lightness and darkness. Though there doesn't seem to be any brightness here; Lennie can spot the one light shining out of the room. It calls him to enter and start talking to Crooks.

For the first time we are seeing Lennie without George. We have a chance to find out what kind of person he really is. George has already told us that Lennie is good to talk to. He seems to let people share their ideas without sticking his opinions in. In that way he is a lot like Slim. In fact, within Crooks' room, Lennie seems to command the same kind of respect that Slim commands within the bunk house. People sort of circle around him.

When Lennie first walks in, Crooks is angry about this "invasion" of his privacy. He says Lennie has no right to be there. The use of the word "right" seems to fit in with one of the books on Crooks' shelf, the California civil code of 1905. Why is that date significant? Perhaps it represents the time when Crooks' father was a landowner and a respected person. Crooks' calling for his rights also echoes similar cries from blacks in the U.S. in the 1930s and since.

NOTE: The Symbol of the Black Man   Steinbeck was always sensitive to the plight of oppressed people, particularly migrant workers and blacks. The character of Crooks gives him an opportunity to make a statement about racial discrimination. Crooks comes from a higher background than most of the ranch hands. His father was not a Southern slave, but a California landowner. He can read, and not just the Bible. He has a dictionary and a law book on his shelf. He points out that his father didn't want him associating with whites. His father was right: through his connection with whites he has become "just a nigger." The way that Lennie changes Crooks' feelings and opinions in the next few pages seems to symbolize Steinbeck's belief that sensitive communication between blacks and whites could help break down discrimination and isolation. Insensitive treatment, such as that illustrated by Curley's wife later in the chapter, puts Crooks "back in his place." Think about these ideas as you read the dialogue in the rest of this chapter.

Have you ever taken part in a conversation where both people were talking at the same time and neither one really heard the other? That's what goes on for the next few pages. Lennie and Crooks are each talking but not listening. Lennie talks about the rabbits, while Crooks fills us in on his history.

Crooks goes rapidly through a series of opposite emotions. First he get excited just from the enjoyment of having someone to talk to. He says, "George can tell you screwy things, and it don't matter. It's just the talking. It's just bein' with another guy. That's all." Then he seems to feel jealous of George and Lennie's companionship and begins to take out on Lennie his bad feelings about his own isolation. He suggests to Lennie that George may not come back from town; he may have deserted Lennie. He presents an image that is at once frightening and foreshadowing: "They'll tie ya up with a collar, like a dog," Crooks says. When he realizes how upset Lennie is, Crooks backs down and eases Lennie's mind about George's safety and loyalty.

NOTE: Lennie and Dogs   Lennie is often compared or linked to animals—mice, horses, dogs, bulls. From here to end of the book, he is most often linked with dogs. Notice Crooks' comment above about the dog collar. The only two dogs we have seen so far in the book are Lennie's puppy and Candy's dog. One of these has already met a tragic end, and Lennie has been warned several times that the puppy may die if it is mistreated. You have seen that nothing good seems to happen to dogs in this book and this should prepare you for the worst to happen to Lennie.

Having gotten his anger and frustration out of his system, Crooks suddenly begins listening to what Lennie is saying about his rabbits and the dream farm. Crooks is scornful about the vision. He has seen hundreds of guys with the same dream come and go, and they never made their dreams come true. Then Candy comes in. He is hesitant at first to enter the black man's room. Crooks pretends to be angry about another invasion, but he is really happy for the company.

Are you noticing what has happened to Crooks' personality and sense of isolation since Lennie has entered his room? Crooks' world seems to be changing for the better. Lennie is like that. He seems to suspend the loneliness of those he comes in contact with.

The Candy who enters Crooks' room is also a different person from the man we saw in earlier chapters. He seems more self-assured and important. Like a businessman, he discusses profits to be gained from raising the rabbits. He becomes really emotional when Crooks mentions his doubts about the farm dream ever coming true. "But we gonna do it now, and don't you make no mistake about that," Candy cries.

Crooks is so impressed by this new Candy that he asks to join them as well. He will work for no pay, just his keep. "I ain't so crippled I can't work like a son-of-a-bitch if I want to," he says. The vision seems to have given new manhood to another misfit in the ranch microcosm.

Curley's wife, the last of the outcasts on the ranch, enters the room next. She announces, accurately, "They left all the weak ones here." The atmosphere in the room quickly changes. Curley's wife is clearly a threat to all of them, even though Lennie is too dumb or love-struck to realize how vulnerable he is. Candy and Crooks try to put her down, but she knows she has the upper hand. It has been a long time since she has been in such a position of power, and she won't give it up easily.

Look at what happens to the three men when Curley's wife confronts them. Candy and Crooks try to act brave but fail. (They become mice instead of men.) Candy begins to mumble again. And, according to Steinbeck, "Crooks had retired into the terrible protective dignity of the Negro. . . . He had reduced himself to nothing."

Having cut down the other two men, she begins in on Lennie. She is not trying to attack him, however. She is trying to seduce him. She says, "I like machines," referring to Lennie's strength. She adds, "I might get a couple of rabbits myself," an obvious sexual comment. Doesn't it seem a little strange to you that Curley's attractive young wife should be after Lennie? He certainly doesn't seem like someone sexy or even interested in sex. Perhaps she sees in Lennie what the others have found, a way out of her loneliness. Or perhaps Steinbeck is showing us that man-woman love in this ranch microcosm is as empty as all the other relationships. There is still a third possibility. Perhaps Steinbeck is trying to re-create an Adam and Eve–type situation. A woman is going to topple the vision of Eden by bringing evil into the world. Whether you see Curley's wife as a real person or as a symbol, one thing is clear: she seems pretty dangerous. Is this another case of foreshadowing? We will find out in the next chapter.

When George comes back to the ranch, he once again takes over control from Lennie. He takes on each of the three men in Crooks' room in turn. He tells Lennie he shouldn't be in the room. He is angry that Candy has told someone else about the dream. And he attacks Crooks in an unspoken way. George seems just as bigoted as the other men on the ranch. Crooks senses this and asks to be removed from his place in the vision.

The three men leave Crooks alone, and the black man seems to remember his crippleness. He begins rubbing liniment on his crooked back. All the hopefulness the outcasts have felt, and the new-found manhood that Lennie has helped them achieve, seem lost.

How have your feelings changed during this chapter? Have you gained new respect for Lennie and lost a little respect for George? Does the vision of the ranch seem closer or farther away than it did at the end of Chapter 3? Think about these questions as you head into Chapter 5.

One thing is interesting to note before you go on. In the play version of *Of Mice and Men*, Chapters 3 and 4 make up the second act of the play. In a three-act play, the first act usually sets up the dramatic situation and introduces the characters. The second act presents slow development of the themes. And the third act brings everything to a climax and conclusion. Think about all the ideas that have been developed in Chapters 3 and 4. What do you think the climax to come in the next act is going to involve? All of the hints Steinbeck has given seem to point to a painful rather than a hopeful ending. Candy's dog has been killed. Lennie has fought with Curley. Lennie hasn't been able to avoid Curley's wife completely. George has gotten very nervous and possessive about the dream. He doesn't want to share it with anyone else. It is almost as if he believes in the superstition that telling someone your wish will keep it from coming true. And Lennie has told everyone about it.

CHAPTER 5: DEATH IN THE BARN

You have been getting lots of hints about bad things that may happen to spoil George and Lennie's dream vision. Here come those bad things—and they are going to come quickly. The first four chapters of *Of Mice and Men* have developed slowly and almost lazily at times. There has been a lot of talk so far and a few brief outbursts of action. The pattern is going to change in these last two chapters. They are shorter than the preceding chapters and packed with more activity.

You wouldn't know about this new pattern from the description of the barn Steinbeck presents at the beginning of Chapter 5: "quiet and humming and lazy and warm." But something seems to contradict this atmosphere right away. Lennie is petting his puppy, but the dog is dead.

You probably aren't surprised that Lennie has killed the puppy. Steinbeck has been foreshadowing this all along. Think back to some of the events that gave us clues—the dead mice in Chapter 1, George's warnings in Chapter 3, the death of Candy's dog in Chapter 3. How do you think that you would respond to the puppy's death if you were Lennie? Lennie's emotions range from anger at the puppy for being so fragile, to worry that George won't let such an irresponsible person tend the rabbits on the farm, to wondering if this killing is bad enough to make him flee to the brush along the riverbank. The one thing Lennie doesn't seem to feel is sadness for the puppy. Once again, Steinbeck seems to be thinking like a biologist. Death occurs in nature. Animals respond to death, but they don't feel regret at having killed. Lennie even tries to act tough about the whole thing. He curses at the dog for getting killed and adds, "This here God damn little son-of-a-bitch wasn't nothing to George."

Things start to get worse. Curley's wife comes into the barn. Lennie quickly buries the puppy and tries to follow George's advice to avoid dealing with her. But she pushes him into a conversation by speaking the almost magic words, "I get lonely." Lennie always seems ready to respond to anyone's need for companionship.

This conversation is a little like the one Lennie and Crooks had in the last chapter. Both people talk, but they don't listen to each other. He tells her about the dead puppy, and she tells him about her sad life. Her words "tumble out in a passion of communication." Once again, Lennie the great listener brings out the talker in other people. She too has dreams that have been cut off. She wanted to be a movie star or a model. Instead she married a man she dislikes, just to spite her mother. She is not living the life of a famous person. In fact, her life is so anonymous that we never even learn her name.

All the time she is talking to Lennie, Curley's wife moves closer to him. Suddenly she realizes that he is not listening to her. She angrily asks him, "Don't you think of nothing but rabbits?" Now Lennie moves close to her. Lennie has to think about his answer. Doesn't this seem a little strange to you? You would figure that since he's been talking about rabbits from the beginning, he knows why he wants to have them. Maybe he's not so much trying to think of an answer as just trying to think of the right words to explain it. He finally answers that he likes to pet nice things. Curley's wife has been worried that Lennie is nuts, but she can understand his love of soft things. She agrees with him, and then invites disaster. She takes Lennie's hand and puts it on her head. We want to warn her and Lennie. But it is too late.

Think back over the different steps that have led up to this point. They have happened almost in slow motion. Curley's wife walks in. Lennie turns away from her. She sits down beside him. She begins moving toward him. Then he moves toward her. She moves away a little and then comes close again. She takes his hand. The movements seem a little like a dance or a fight, don't they?

Suddenly we are in fast motion, and the dance becomes a dance of death. Curley's wife screams and struggles. Lennie, afraid of what George will say, tries to quiet her forcefully and eventually breaks her neck. Throughout the description of the struggle and for the next few pages, Steinbeck uses lots of animal images to describe Lennie's actions. He paws the hay and listens to "the cry of men." He crouches and listens like a frightened beast. Perhaps Steinbeck is trying to show us that Lennie is more an animal than a person.

NOTE: The Nonhuman Side of Lennie   Lennie has been compared to various animals since the first chapter in the book. Yet his animal nature never really seemed dangerous before. Now we are struck with the idea that Lennie cannot fit in human society; he is a more primitive form of life. This idea will be reinforced by Slim's statement at the end of this chapter that if Lennie is left alive he will be strapped down and put in a cage.

Steinbeck created a similar character in his earlier novel, *The Pastures of Heaven*. The character's name was Tularecito. People try to "civilize" Tularecito by sending him to school and beating him until he behaves like a normal boy. But he never does. Instead he strikes back violently when he thinks people are trying to block him from communicating with his real ancestors, the gnomes who live within nature. You might want to read "The Origin of Tularecito" in *The Pastures of Heaven* and see if he is a model for Lennie.

After the killing, everything becomes still and quiet. Slim's dog is the first one to sense death in the air, and she cringes in with her puppies. Meanwhile Curley's wife lies in the barn. She looks more peaceful and lovelier than ever before. In death, she has regained her innocence.

Then all hell breaks loose. Candy discovers the body and brings George. They discuss what will happen to Lennie now, but Candy is more interested in their dream. He says that he and George could still get "that little place" and "live nice there." George doesn't even bother to answer. Without Lennie to keep reminding him to discuss the dream and to keep making him feel needed, the dream cannot come true. George has become just another lonely, rootless ranch hand. He says, "I'll work my month an' I'll take my fifty bucks an' I'll stay all night in some lousy cat house." Remember, these are the same words he used to describe the "loneliest guys in the world" in Chapter 1. Lennie is no longer going to be there to chime in, "But not us. . . . Because I got you to look after me, and you got me to look after you!"

What do you think about this exchange between Candy and George? Some readers think that it is powerful and emotional; others think that it is overly sentimental. Do you think the exchange is really necessary to get across Steinbeck's message about loneliness being at the heart of life in the 1930s? Or do you think the author is trying to knock you over the head with the message? Your opinion here will probably determine whether or not you like *Of Mice and Men*.

The action continues with the other ranch hands arriving on the scene and setting up a search party (or lynching party) to find Lennie and bring him to "justice." Curley is all for lynching Lennie or shooting him in the guts. After all, Curley has his manhood to defend. Lennie has beaten him in a fight and has now taken away his wife. Slim suggests to George that he not allow Lennie to be captured and caged like an animal (see the previous note). But George already knows this. And we suspect that it was George who stole Carlson's Luger, the gun that was used to kill Candy's dog.

The chapter draws to a close. Candy, who has been left behind, lies down on the hay and covers his eyes with his arm. This is the same pose his dog used to take. There is more death in the air.

CHAPTER 6: DEATH AT THE RIVER

The final scene is set in the same place as the first scene, along the banks of the Salinas River. Even the time of day is almost the same. The story has now made a full circle. The location may be the same, but Steinbeck's description of the setting is quite different. Look carefully for those differences. Look particularly for images of death. There are lots of them.

George had always intended that the brush along the riverbank be a haven for Lennie and him should anything go wrong. But this "new" place doesn't seem so safe. Instead of lizards, rabbits, and deer, we see a water snake gliding along like a submarine, looking for prey. The snake becomes the victim of a heron that "lanced down and plucked it out by the head, and the beak swallowed the little snake while its tail waved frantically." We also saw a heron in the first scene, but it was flying away, not attacking. Instead of "a little wind," we now have a "rush of wind" that gusts through the trees. The leaves are no longer green; they are brown and rotting.

Just as in Chapter 1, man (Lennie) invades nature. But this time Lennie doesn't drink with trust and glee. He barely touches his lips to the water. Lennie has come to wait for George and reassurance that everything will be okay.

As we have seen, Steinbeck's setting descriptions at the beginning of each chapter not only set the scene but create atmosphere as well. The atmosphere here is obviously one of trouble and death.

Even Lennie senses that he has done something really bad this time. Lennie may not be fully human, but his primitive human conscience begins to trouble him. He is haunted by two strange visions. First his Aunt Clara appears to accuse him of not listening to George and of making George's life miserable. She presents Lennie with one of his alternatives—going off by himself. Then Aunt Clara fades away and is replaced by a giant rabbit that says Lennie "ain't fit to lick the boots of no rabbit." The rabbit suggests another alternative—getting beaten by George or deserted by him. Lennie begins to cry for George, and his friend suddenly appears.

NOTE: The Visions   Lennie's two visions give us an interesting insight into his feelings of guilt. Neither Aunt Clara nor the giant rabbit mentions the killing of the girl or the puppy. Lennie isn't really guilty of murder because he isn't responsible for his actions. Lennie's guilt lies more in his failure to live up to the human side of his character, his desire for friendship and a sense of responsibility.

It is interesting that neither vision is included in the play version of *Of Mice and Men*. Perhaps Steinbeck felt that a play audience would not understand or appreciate the presentation of Lennie's lack of guilt.

George and Lennie have two different stories that they share and repeat throughout the book. One involves the vision of the farm; the other is George's mock attack on Lennie as someone who ruins the "good life" he could have. Now Lennie wants to hear the second story. It would convince him that George still wants him around. George starts the attack, but he can't carry it off. He knows that soon Lennie won't be around and he will be forced to live that not-so-good life. So George begins telling the first story instead. Lennie doesn't seem to notice. He just joins in where he always does.

Meanwhile George is placing Carlson's Luger behind Lennie's ear, just where Carlson said he would shoot Curley's dog. George hesitates to pull the trigger. He tells Lennie to look across the river where he can "almost see" the farm. That's how close the vision seemed to him just a day ago. When the voices of the other men sound close by, George shoots.

George has one more act to carry out before the

story ends. He lies about Lennie's death, saying that his friend was going to shoot him. Why does George lie? The most logical reason is that George is a survivor. If he admitted that he had stolen Carlson's Luger, he would have been suspect around the ranch from now on. If he admitted that he shot Lennie in cold blood, he would have been labeled a murderer by some. George chooses to go on living with his own feelings. Do you think he feels guilty about killing Lennie? Probably not. Instead, he just feels empty.

The last words in the book are left to Slim and Carlson, the two opposite poles of humanity on the ranch. Slim compassionately says, "You hadda, George." Carlson coldly comments, "Now what the hell ya suppose is eatin' them two guys?" That Steinbeck chooses to leave us with Carlson's message instead of Slim's shows us that he sees the world as a cold, lonely place.

This entire last part is not included in the play version of *Of Mice and Men*. The play ends with Lennie's death. The play ending is moving and a little sentimental. The novel ending is pretty cynical. Which version do you think is more satisfying? Your answer may depend on whether you are sitting in an audience or reading a book. A playwright wants to get a huge round of applause after a performance. A novelist wants to leave the audience in a thoughtful mood. With his two versions of *Of Mice and Men*, Steinbeck was able to try out both methods.

A STEP BEYOND

Tests and Answers

TESTS

Test 1

1. We gain an early insight into Lennie's
   problem when
   A. he admits to George that he can't read
      traffic signs
   B. we learn about the dead mouse in his
      pocket
   C. he forgets his own name

2. When Steinbeck tells us that Lennie likes to
   pet things, he is using the technique of
   A. narration
   B. graphic description
   C. foreshadowing

3. George can make Lennie feel bad by
   A. telling what a burden Lennie is to him
   B. teasing him about the rabbit farm
   C. refusing to give him any spending
      money

4. George and Lennie felt that they were
   different from other itinerant ranch hands
   because they
   A. had desirable skills
   B. liked to put roots down in one place
   C. could look after each other

5. Milton and Small were _____
   A. the last names of George and Lennie
   B. the agents who supplied itinerant workers for ranch jobs
   C. the two mule skinners on the ranch

6. George explained Lennie's problem to everyone by saying _____
   A. he had been the victim of a childhood disease
   B. he had been kicked in the head by a horse
   C. his parents had kept him out of school

7. In his first meeting with both men, Curley was irritated because _____
   A. George did all the talking
   B. Lennie didn't show him the proper respect
   C. they seemed incompetent

8. The swamper characterized Curley's new bride as _____
   A. a whiner
   B. a frustrated actress
   C. a tart

9. One of the important developments of the plot was introduced when _____
   A. we learn that Slim's dog had a litter of pups
   B. Carlson makes his entrance
   C. Slim asks George and Lennie to join his work crew

10. The story of Lennie's near disaster in the   _____
    town of Weed
    A. added to our sympathy for him
    B. exacerbated Curley's bitterness toward
       both men
    C. prepared us for the violence which lay
       ahead

11. In many ways, Lennie is the central character in the
    book. Nearly all of the action and characters revolve
    around him. Discuss this idea.

12. Where does the title of the book come from? Why is the
    title appropriate?

13. Discuss how the ranch in *Of Mice and Men* is a micro-
    cosm of American society as a whole.

14. Steinbeck had originally planned to call the book *Some-
    thing That Happened*. Explain why. Discuss which title
    you like best.

15. Discuss why the other characters in the book are sus-
    picious or skeptical about the relationship between
    George and Lennie.

Test 2

1. The shooting of Candy's dog is an example   _____
   of Steinbeck's

   A. sensitivity toward all of God's creatures
   B. fondness for symbolism
   C. propensity for mood changes

2. When Lennie thought of the idyllic future   _____
   on their own farm, he said,
   A. "I'll save alla my dollahs for that,
      George."
   B. "We could live off the fatta the lan' "
   C. "Ain't nobody gonna stan' in our way"

3. Curley was   _____
      I. blackmailed into lying about his
         broken hand
     II. a bully who liked to provoke fights
    III. outraged when he thought Lennie
         had been laughing at him
   A. I and II only   B. I and III only
      C. I, II, and III

4. The lowest man in the ranch hierarchy was   _____
   A. Candy, the swamper
   B. Crooks, the stable buck
   C. Bill Tenner, the mule skinner

5. When Crooks heard about the plans for a   _____
   farm, he
   A. asked for additional details immediately
   B. belittled them
   C. offered to join in the project

6. Lennie's puppy died when   _____
   A. Carlson ran it over
   B. Curley drowned it
   C. Lennie hit it

7. Curley's wife precipitated her own death by   _____
   A. enticing Lennie down to the river bank
   B. inviting Lennie to stroke her hair
   C. giving Lennie the eye in front of her
      husband

8. "Ever' body knowed you'd mess things up" ____
was George's statement to
   A. Lennie before he pulled the trigger
   B. Candy when he revealed their "secret"
      plans about the farm
   C. the dead body of Curley's wife

9. While waiting at the river bank for George, ____
Lennie conjured up a vision of
   A. his Aunt Clara
   B. the posse that was coming to hang him
   C. the woman in the red dress in Weed

10. George felt that he had to carry out the ____
execution
   A. as retribution for Lennie's crime
   B. before the other men would get to
      Lennie
   C. since Lennie had jeopardized their future

11. Steinbeck has said he intended the book to be a play in
novel form. Describe ways in which the novel is similar
to a play.

12. Foreshadowing is an important part of Steinbeck's technique. Describe several instances of foreshadowing that
are presented in the book.

13. What do George and Lennie mean when they say they
want "to live off the fat of the land"?

14. Choose one of the following minor characters and
explain what his or her purpose is in the novel: Slim,
Curley, Whit, Curley's wife.

15. The play form of *Of Mice and Men* ends with George
shooting Lennie. The novel continues for several more
pages. Discuss what Steinbeck is saying in those last
pages of the book.

ANSWERS

Test 1

1. B   **2.** C   **3.** A   **4.** B   **5.** A   **6.** B
7. A   **8.** C   **9.** A   **10.** C

11. Lennie is always at the center of the action of the story. Even when he is not on the scene, he is being talked about by the other characters, for example, when George and Slim talk in Chapter 3. Nearly all of the characters interact with Lennie. Since we as readers feel so sympathetic toward Lennie throughout the book, we generally measure the other characters by their responses to Lennie. We respect George for his devotion to a partner who must often seem a burden to him. We hate Curley for his picking on Lennie. We almost feel that Curley's wife got what she deserved for trying to seduce Lennie. Lennie brings out both the best and worst in the people he deals with.

Lennie is also the central figure in forming and maintaining the dream vision that is at the heart of the novel. Lennie pushes George into articulating the vision. It seems that George has to keep being reminded so that he won't lose sight of this better future. Maybe this is because George could live a normal ranch life, but Lennie couldn't. If George and Lennie are to stay together, they must find a new life on their own, away from other people. Perhaps the clearest indication of Lennie's importance to the novel is that without Lennie, the dream vision withers and dies.

12. The origin of the title was explained earlier in the discussion of themes. According to the Robert Burns poem from which the title is taken, the best laid schemes of both mice and men often go astray. George and Lennie have a scheme of their own that promises joy. But, as in the poem, it will go astray and leave nothing but grief and pain behind. The images of mice and men are also central to the book. The characters who link themselves with the scheme—George, Lennie, Candy, Crooks—are mice who want to be men. They are nobodies who want to find importance and self-respect. For a while, in the third and fourth chapters, these mice are elevated to manhood. George has a real place in mind; Lennie knows the colors of his rabbits; Candy becomes a businessman counting his profits; and Crooks no longer feels like a cripple. But in the end micehood prevails. George will live the lonely life of a ranch hand; Lennie is dead; Candy is left behind when the posse goes out after Lennie; and Crooks feels the need for his liniment.

13. The early 1930s was a time of poverty, homelessness, and pain in the United States. Families were breaking apart. Violence in the form of labor strikes and an impending world war was in the air. All of these feelings are mirrored in the ranch of *Of Mice and Men*. The ranch is filled with characters who are more symbolic than real. As such, they represent various aspects of American society in the 1930s. George and Lennie are the working class looking for a better life but unable to overcome the system that holds them down. Candy is old age, no longer respected as in the past but instead pushed aside. Crooks is the black man turned into a "nigger" and isolated from the rest of society. Curley's wife shows us that love has become empty and is often replaced by lust.

Steinbeck's style in the novel also indicates that he intended the book to be more of an allegory than a narration, and his ranch to be more of a microcosm than a real place. His themes are obvious and his characterizations are only sketchily developed. Steinbeck is making a social statement in the book while he tells a story.

14. By titling the book *Something That Happened*, Steinbeck would have demonstrated his feeling that there is no power controlling what happens in this world. Things just happen. Nature goes on, bringing with it life and death. People come into the world and go out of it, and they are only barely noticed. Life is fairly mechanical. Throughout the novel there is a sense of the ending's being inevitable. There is no way for George and Lennie to prevent the impending tragedy. In that sense, the events that occur are just "some things that happen."

The title *Of Mice and Men* adds to this view. The new title illustrates that we will still strive to develop schemes to overcome our small role in the universe. We will build hopes to find a better world. But in the end we will fail. The first title would give readers a sense of emptiness; the second title gives them a feeling of pain.

15. Faced with the poverty and emptiness of their lives, most of the people on the ranch have isolated themselves from others. People are always moving into and out of their lives, such as the cleanness freak whose bunk George takes over or the former ranch hand who wrote the letter to the magazine. Their aloneness is a way of protecting themselves. The most obvious example of this is Crooks. He has been forced to live alone, but he has turned his lean-to into a personal sanctum. The characters seem to know that opening themselves up to relationships with others can expose them to the danger of being rejected or of the pain of losing a friend. Perhaps these feelings are what motivate Crooks to frighten Lennie with his story of George's deserting him in Chapter 4.

Having this mentality, the characters are naturally suspicious of George and Lennie's partnership. Why are these two men traveling together? Why are they looking for permanence in the vision of a farm of their own? They feel, like the boss, that George must be out to exploit Lennie. Or they feel, like Curley's wife, that the relationship is just a front.

In the end, the skeptics turn out to be right. Relationships in the world of the ranch are doomed to failure.

Test 2

1. B   **2.** B   **3.** C   **4.** B   **5.** B   **6.** C   **7.** B
8. C   **9.** A   **10.** B

11. There are lots of playlike characteristics in the novel. In fact, when the play was first staged, nearly 85 percent of it was taken directly from the novel. For one thing, each chapter opens with a setting description that sounds a lot like stage directions. For another, the book consists mostly of dialogue. Also, Steinbeck doesn't really describe the characters; he lets them reveal themselves through their words and actions. In addition the action takes place over a very short period of time in one central location. And the plot develops a step at a time right before our eyes, with the narrator not commenting on events before they happen. These are all play characteristics, not those of most novels. Even the actions that occur seem "staged." For example, Curley and Lennie's fight seems to be a duel on stage, and Lennie and Curley's wife seem to be dancing together before she is killed (see the description of this "dance" in the analysis of Chapter 5 of this guide). Novels are usually noted for extended descriptions, development of characterizations, and the flowing quality of their language. Plays are noted for the directness of language and characterizations. If these characteristics are typical, *Of Mice and Men* seems to have more in common with plays than novels.

12. One of the ways Steinbeck holds the events of the book together and moves the plot is through the use of foreshadowing. Lennie's trouble in Weed foreshadows his killing of Curley's wife. Candy's dog is shot in the same way and with the same weapon with which Lennie will be killed. George's warnings about not fooling around with Curley or Curley's wife turn out to be prophetic. His warnings that Lennie may kill the puppy if he handles it too much also turn out to be accurate.

Steinbeck's use of foreshadowing is not only a plot device; it is also a stylistic tool. Foreshadowing builds up drama. As the events and warnings accumulate, we readers are put on the edge of our seats waiting for the tragic event that must be coming. In that sense, Lennie's killing at the end is not so much a climax for us as a release from our anticipation of the event. It is almost a relief to feel sadness instead of worry at the end of the book.

13. As members of the working class and as ranch hands, George and Lennie are almost servants of the land. Like Adam and Eve after eating the apple, they must work for their daily bread instead of experiencing the joys of the Garden of Eden before the fall from grace. They long for a return to Eden. They want to be owners. They want the land to be their servant and to give them something freely. Their paradise need be only a few acres and a few animals, including rabbits. They want to run their own lives for a change and not have to work so hard just to get by. This is what the image of "living off the fat of the land" means. Unfortunately, in the time of the Depression, the land isn't fat. There isn't very much to live off of.

14. All of the characters in the novel have been discussed in detail in The Characters section of this guide (pages 10–22) and in the analyses of Chapters 2 and 5. You might want to study these discussions to help develop your essay for this topic.

15. The play form of *Of Mice and Men* ends on a high dramatic note—George's shooting of Lennie, a tragedy and great show of love on George's part. The audience is left in a very emotional mood. In the novel, Steinbeck wants to get beyond the emotion. He wants to show that life will go on for George and the other characters. George's life will be emptier now, but it will continue. George illustrates this by lying about Lennie's death. He could have made a grand gesture and described how he killed Lennie as a sign of love. But he chooses not to. Steinbeck seems to be saying that loneliness and not love is the dominant feeling in the world of *Of Mice and Men*. He lets Carlson express the last thought in the book, one filled with cynicism. Mice, not men, live in this world.

Term Paper Ideas

You may want to write a theme or term paper based on ideas presented in *Of Mice and Men* or suggested by the book. Here is a list of topics to help you plan your paper. The topics are arranged in four categories—characterization, symbolism, style or technique, and theme.

Characterization

1. Discuss Lennie as both man and animal.

2. Examine the childlike qualities in Lennie.

3. Discuss why Candy and Crooks are the only two ranch hands who want to be part of George and Lennie's dream.

4. Examine the contrasting characters of Slim and Carlson.

5. Examine the roles of one or more minor characters.

6. Discuss the suitability of the various characters' names.

7. Describe ways that Steinbeck presents pairs of characters who complement each other.

Symbolism

1. Describe how the novel is related to the Cain and Abel story in the Bible.

2. Describe ways that Lennie and George's vision parallels the search for the Holy Grail.

3. Describe and explain the large number of hand references in the novel.

4. Discuss the view of women expressed in the novel.

5. Explain the importance of rabbits to Lennie.

6. Examine Candy and Crooks as symbols of isolation.

7. Discuss light and dark imagery in the novel.

Style or Technique

1. Discuss the parallels between the killing of Candy's dog and Lennie.

2. Examine Steinbeck's use or overuse of foreshadowing.

3. Describe the poetic qualities of Steinbeck's language.

4. Decide whether the book is genuinely moving or overly sentimental, and back up your opinion.

5. Discuss the purpose and effect of the setting descriptions that open each chapter in the book.

6. Examine the playlike qualities of the novel. In what ways is it more like a play than a novel?

7. Contrast the novel and play versions of *Of Mice and Men*. What are some major differences between the two forms of the story? Why has Steinbeck made these differences?

Theme

1. Discuss the theme of loneliness in the novel.

2. Examine George and Lennie as a single two-sided character.

3. Describe the symbiotic relationship between George and Lennie.

4. Discuss what George's life would be like without Lennie, and Lennie's without George.

5. Examine the concept of the ranch as a microcosm of American society.

6. Discuss George's motives in killing Lennie.

7. What is love like in the novel? Discuss the lack of what we would consider normal, loving relationships.

8. Describe the book as a response to the Great Depression of the 1930s.

9. Discuss the place of man within nature as expressed in the novel.

Further Reading

CRITICAL WORKS

Here are some books that deal wholly or in part with the writing of John Steinbeck. You might want to read through several of them to get some added insights into Steinbeck's style and themes and into *Of Mice and Men*.

Astro, Richard, and Tetsumaro Hayashi. *Steinbeck: The Man and His Work.* Corvallis, Ore.: Oregon State University Press, 1971.

This is a collection of essays written by members of The John Steinbeck Society and delivered at a conference in 1970. The essays deal with many different aspects of Steinbeck's work. You'll probably be the most interested in "John Steinbeck: A Reminiscence" written by Steinbeck's longtime friend Webster Street (pp. 35–42) and "Escape and Commitment: Two Poles of the Steinbeck Hero" by Peter Lisca (pp. 75–88).

French, Warren. *John Steinbeck.* New York: Twayne Publishers, 1961.

This book is an easy-to-read study of Steinbeck's life and works up to 1960. One chapter is devoted to *Of Mice and Men*. It also contains a good bibliography of critical works about Steinbeck.

Kazin, Alfred. *On Native Grounds.* New York: Reynal, 1942.

This is a study of American writers of the 1930s by an important literary critic. Kazin is very critical of *Of Mice and Men*. He feels it is too simple to convey the seriousness of its themes, and too sentimental.

Levant, Howard. *The Novels of John Steinbeck: A Critical Study*. Columbia, Mo.: University of Missouri Press, 1974.

This study of all the major works of Steinbeck is thorough, but a little difficult to read. Levant is also critical of *Of Mice and Men* and considers the play-novelette form too limiting for developing complete characters and themes.

Lisca, Peter. *John Steinbeck, Nature and Myth*. New York: Thomas Y. Crowell, 1978.

This is an interesting, readable study that relates Steinbeck's themes with his style.

————. *The Wide World of John Steinbeck*. New Brunswick, N.J.: Rutgers University Press, 1958.

This is a close reading of all of Steinbeck's works up to 1958. It is one of the most famous books on Steinbeck's writing.

Moore, Harry T. *The Novels of John Steinbeck*. Chicago: Normandie House, 1939.

This is the first important study of Steinbeck's life and works. It is valuable because it concentrates on only the early novels, so more attention is given to *Of Mice and Men* than in later critical works.

Steinbeck, Elaine, and Robert Wallsten. *Steinbeck: A Life in Letters*. New York: Viking, 1975.

This is the collected letters of John Steinbeck organized chronologically. Steinbeck wrote lots of letters, and the book is nearly 900 pages long. The letters provide an insight into Steinbeck's feelings and personal life that you won't find anywhere else.

Tedlock, E. W., Jr., and C. V. Wicker, eds. *Steinbeck and His Critics, A Record of Twenty-Five Years*. Albuquerque: University of New Mexico Press, 1957.

This is another must for serious study of Steinbeck's writing. The book contains critical essays by Steinbeck on his own writing, and by seventeen other writers commenting on Steinbeck's work.

AUTHOR'S OTHER WORKS

Here is a bibliography of all of Steinbeck's major works arranged in chronological order.

Cup of Gold   (novel), 1929.

The Pastures of Heaven   (novel), 1932.

To a God Unknown   (novel), 1933.

The Red Pony   (four-part novella), 1933.

''The Murder''   (short story), 1934.

Tortilla Flat   (novel), 1935.

In Dubious Battle   (novel), 1936.

Of Mice and Men   (novel and play), 1937.

The Long Valley   (short-story collection), 1938.

The Grapes of Wrath   (novel), 1939.

The Sea of Cortez   (biological study written with Ed Ricketts), 1941.

The Forgotten Village   (film and illustrated book about a Mexican village), 1941.

Bombs Away   (nonfiction propaganda book written for Army Air Force), 1942.

The Moon Is Down   (play-novelette), 1942.

Lifeboat   (filmscript), 1944.

Cannery Row   (novel), 1945.

The Wayward Bus   (novel), 1947.

The Pearl   (novella), 1947.

A Russian Journal   (nonfiction account of a trip to Russia), 1948.

Burning Bright   (play-novelette), 1950.

Viva Zapata   (filmscript), 1950.

The Log from the Sea of Cortez (nonfiction account of the 1940 expedition to Mexico), 1951.

East of Eden (novel), 1952.

Sweet Thursday (novel), 1954.

Once There Was a War (collected war correspondence from World War II), 1959.

The Winter of Our Discontent (novel), 1961.

Travels with Charley in Search of America (nonfiction account of a cross-country trip), 1962.

America and Americans (nonfiction), 1968.

The Critics

Here are some brief excerpts taken from the writings of several major literary critics. The excerpts deal with aspects of Steinbeck's style, purpose, themes, and characterization in *Of Mice and Men*. The comments may help you develop some new ideas about the book. You might want to use them when you write your own themes.

On Theme:

What gives the book solidity in the reader's mind and real stature among Steinbeck's works is the empathy created by George and Lennie in their striving to overcome essential human loneliness. The story is set, in the first words of the book, 'A few miles south of Soledad,' an actual place in California whose Spanish name means both loneliness and a lonely place.

—Peter Lisca, *John Steinbeck, Nature and Myth*, 1978

On George:

George could, of course, have killed Lennie simply to protect the giant brute from the mob; but, since Lennie doesn't know what is going on anyway, it is easy to oversentimentalize George's motives. Actually he has reasons of his own for pulling the trigger. Steinbeck makes it clear that George has tremendous difficulty bringing himself to destroy Lennie, although Lennie will not even know what has happened. What George is actually trying to kill is not Lennie, who is only a shell and a doomed one at that, but something in himself.

—Warren French, *John Steinbeck*, 1961

On Form and Structure:

The climax is doubled, a pairing of opposites. . . . The climax pairs an exploration of the ambiguity of love in the rigid contrast between the motives that activate Curley's wife and George. Curley's wife wants to use Lennie to show her hatred for Curley; George shoots Lennie out of real affection for him. The attempted seduction balances the knowing murder; both are disastrous expressions of love. Lennie is the unknowing center of design in both halves of this climax. Steinbeck's control is all too evident. There is not much sense of dramatic illumination because the quality of the paired climax is that of a mechanical problem of joining two parallels. Lennie's necessary passivity enforces the quality of a mechanical design. He is only the man to whom things happen. Being so limited, he is incapable of providing that sudden widening insight which alone justifies an artist's extreme dependence on a rigid design. Therefore, in general, *Of Mice and Men* remains a simple anecdote.

—Howard Levant, *The Novels of John Steinbeck: A Critical Study*, 1974

On Steinbeck's Dialogue:

There is a curious thing that has always seemed to run through John's writing. This is his fondness for spontaneous human expression, as, for instance, when someone gets in a jam and says something, and you think, 'Well, that's a hell of a thing to say.' In many cases, say at the end of *The Red Pony* and throughout *In Dubious Battle,* John relies on the truth of spontaneous human reaction in speech. Critics might contend that he made up these passages, but a good many times I think he took them right from what people told him, because when you talked to John, you were conscious that he knew you a great deal better than you would ever know him.

—Webster Street, in *Steinbeck: The Man and His Work*, 1971